Empty
Ba

MIKE ROOT

Empty Baskets

Offering Your Life as Worship

COLLEGE PRESS
PUBLISHING COMPANY
Joplin, Missouri

International Standard Book Number   0-89900-866-6

264 S
R

1 Worship   2 Stewardship

DEDICATION

It is with great joy and humility that I dedicate *Empty Baskets* to a family of Christians who have loved my family and me in a very special way the last two years. They have smothered us with encouragement, taken us in like long-lost family members, and provided healing that we were sent to give to them. They have restored my faith in friendship, spiritual families, and especially spiritual leadership. I thank God for calling us to be with this wonderful family of His. With love and deep appreciation, I dedicate this book to the shepherds and members of the Antioch Church of Christ in Antioch, Tennessee. May God give us many years to glorify Him together.

TABLE OF CONTENTS

INTRODUCTION

It was my first fatality. I was so new that the officers I was trying to minister to hadn't figured out if I was a "good guy" or an alien invader sent from Headquarters to spy on them. I was a volunteer Police Chaplain with a shiny new badge, a briefcase full of cop toys, and a boatload full of anxiety. Hearing the sergeant's voice on the radio calling for "Chaplain 8 to respond to the 9-F" nearly caused the boat to capsize.

I had been riding with one of the older, more experienced officers that night, and I was really making some headway in terms of building a relationship. They'd never had a chaplain before and there was no policy about using chaplains, so we were only effective to the extent that we could build trust and develop a need for us. I was about to be thrust into the vortex of real-life street survival, and I'd have to prove myself worthy of inclusion into the closed world of police work.

I'll never forget the sight of the accident scene in the distance as we came over the hill. Red emergency lights flashed across four lanes of highway and spread into the woods on the left side of the road. It was amazing. There were police cruisers galore along with three ambulances and a couple of fire engines. Then to give the whole scene a base of color, road flares burned fluorescent all over the place, like giant Fourth of July sparklers. Headlights and spotlights cast weird shadows all around, and the yellow vehicle flashers gave everything the look of being on fire. Officers scurried around or directed traffic using their huge five-celled flashlights. If I hadn't been so frightened by the prospects of walking into the middle of all that, it might have looked like something from Mardi Gras or a Disney light show.

The sergeant came over to me as soon as I stepped from the cruiser. He was a very religious man and the only person I knew who was excited about having a chaplain — before he ever met me. He explained the situation to me. Two cars started racing each other down the road. As the car on the inside lane passed the car in the outside lane, and began to change lanes to get in front of him, he lost control of his car and continued off the road, across the shoulder and into the woods. Even though the car crashed into a tree, both the occupants walked away without a scratch. The problem was the sixteen-year-old boy, who had been riding his bike down the shoulder of the road. They plowed into him and killed him instantly. His twisted body lay in the creek that flowed just a few yards from the edge of the road.

It was quite an experience for me. I didn't have time to reflect on the sad tragedy until much later. After being totally briefed on the situation, I was immediately sent to deal with the little boy's parents who were in the crowd of spectators and screaming to know if it was their boy. We didn't have any identification on the boy and we weren't about to start letting people walk up and take a look at the body. I had to physically restrain them from charging through the police barricade and going to see if it was their son. It was a long and tense situation, and I had to do some quick thinking on my feet. Finally, when we were reasonably sure who he was, we let the boy's father identify the body before it was placed into the ambulance.

Much later, after helping the family get back to their home and arranging for their pastor to come help them, I was able to return to the crime scene. It was a crime scene because the driver of the car was intoxicated and had a previous conviction for vehicular manslaughter, which is what he was charged with this time. I used this time to further my education. I was especially fascinated by the work of the Accident Investigation Officer. He showed me several very interesting things, like how he would use the speedometer plate to prove how fast the car was going when it struck the tree. The speedometer pin struck the plate upon impact and left traces of fluorescent paint on the MPH numbers. That, along with the tire marks, would prove that the driver was drastically over the speed limit at the time of the accident.

He also explained to me what all the paint marks on the road meant. These marks were placed there by the investigating officer to facilitate measuring and picture taking. The paint would stay there for several days in case they needed to return later and do some further investigative work.

The most intriguing mark on the road involved three letters with an arrow pointing off the road. They were POI. They stood for "Point Of Impact." It marked, for measuring and photographic purposes, the exact spot where the vehicle struck the boy on the bicycle and ended his short life. What started out as a quick trip to a pizza parlor ended on a gravel shoulder marked POI.

What a difference that POI made. A little boy's life was snuffed out; a family was swamped by grief; a thoughtless young man was on his way to prison; his family was hurting; a school full of children were struggling to understand why their friend wasn't coming back; a community and its traffic were disrupted; a brand new Police Chaplain was initiated; and a bunch of hardened cops struggled with sadness, because even the most calloused cop drops his defenses when cases involve children. Yes, that was some Point Of Impact!

That road was a main artery of travel for my family and me. I can personally testify that the fluorescent orange paint remained on the asphalt for a long time. It became a Point of Impact for me over and over again. Not only did it remind me of that first call for me as a Police Chaplain, but it reminded me of the time when I was walking down the side of the road, when I was only fifteen, and I was struck by a pickup truck.

There was a great deal of discussion after my accident as to whether I was walking on the road, which would have placed at least some of the fault on me, or whether the driver of the truck went off the road and struck me. An accurate POI was crucial in determining who was at fault. Fortunately, I wasn't walking alone, so I had a witness who could corroborate where I believed the POI to be. That made a huge difference when it came time to settle hospital bills and the other things we settled out of court. (My week in the hospital and broken hip were worth $1300 back in 1966 and the hospital bill was just over $600. That wouldn't repair a dented fender today!)

In terms of an accurate determination of facts and an investigation of basic truth, few things are more important than having an exact POI. The more life changing the collision, the more important it is to know where the Point Of Impact is.

If worship is a meeting, an intentional collision between man and God, where's the POI? Is it a series of POI's or a scheduled, weekly event? Is it a time and place or an attitude? Is it being "impacted" or is it "impacting others?" Is it a planned, orchestrated experience bracketed by opening and closing prayers, and designed to make you "encounter God," or is it a "cup of cold water" given in the name of Jesus?

Maybe the Point of Impact is the conviction and conversion of a soul that once was lost and now is found. Maybe it's the decision to offer up one's life as a continual sacrifice to God — a sacrifice that is total, never ending, and always glorifies God. Maybe the POI is simply the starting point of what should be a life given in obedience to God — a life of worship to Him.

Then again, most people would say that the POI of worship takes place at 11:00 A.M. at their church building every Sunday morning. It's the collision everyone walks away from.

What is worship? Is it a place, a time, an event, a performance, an experience, and a duty? Is it something you go to and leave? Is it an encounter with God in a special way other than what's normal? Is it a series of acts, a set of rituals, a formal occasion, and a "payback" for God's goodness to us? Is it something to be endured, checked off, attended, and used as a criterion for faithfulness and holiness? Can you go to heaven if you don't go to church? Is there a difference between worship and the assembly of saints? Is there any example in the New Testament of an assembly that remotely looks like ours? Is there a bigger but simpler picture of New Testament worship that we haven't seen?

For Christians, our Point of Impact is when our hearts collide with the Crucified Christ. Worship is what we agree — what we are compelled — to give to Him because of His great love and sacrifice for us. Our worship to Him must be no less than His love for us!

CHAPTER ONE
Stewards of Truth

Paul was thrown off his "high horse" by Jesus. Talk about a clear "Point Of Impact" — that was one! Even though he had seen the Light, he was struck blind and told to go into the city and wait. That must have been a tough three-day wait for Paul. My impression of Paul from Scripture is that he was a Type A personality (in a stereotypically negative sense), at least at that time in his life. He was a "let's-get-it-done-now" kind of guy. He was conscientious, driven, and dedicated to the truth — as he understood it. There was nothing half-hearted about him. If Judaism was right, then this Jesus Movement was wrong and needed to be squashed, and he was just the man to do it. But now, here he was, convicted of sin and guilty of fighting against God, fasting and praying for guidance, blind as a bat and with no idea how long it would be until he found out what he needed to do to get things right with God.

The Bible doesn't tell us what he said or did, but I suspect that when God healed him of blindness through Ananias and challenged him with, "And now why do you delay? Arise, and be baptized, and wash away your sins, calling on His name," he jumped for joy. I can see him dragging Ananias to the nearest pool of water and saying, "Let's do it now! I've got a lot of work to do for the Lord!" (Acts 22:6-16).

The Bible says that he joined with the disciples in Damascus, "and immediately he *began* to proclaim Jesus in the synagogues, saying, 'He is the Son of God.'" (Acts 9:19-20). From that moment on he gave his life to Jesus, which means he was totally and absolutely committed to living for Him. On three different mission trips he started churches all over the known world. He suffered every conceivable kind of hardship in his service to Jesus. Just read his resume of experiences in 2 Corinthians 11:23-33 the next time you think living for Jesus has been hard for you, and it will put things into a completely different light. Yet even with all the beatings, sufferings, and other hardships he mentions, it was his concern for the churches that he called a "daily pressure," and seemed to indicate that it was the heaviest burden.

His commitment was so strong that he could "count all things to be loss in view of the surpassing value of knowing Christ Jesus my Lord, for whom I have suffered the loss of all things, and count them but rubbish in order that I may gain Christ" (Phil 3:8). His fearless faith caused him to actually debate with himself as to whether or not it was better for him to die and be with Jesus or stay and help His church! Being with Jesus, he said, was clearly better, but doing His will was what was needed (Phil 1:21-26). So he traveled, testified, was imprisoned, wrote letters to churches, shared the gospel with everyone he could, and praised God for the opportunity to work for Him in weakness with a "thorn in the flesh" (2 Cor 12:7-10). According to historical tradition he was executed in Rome for his faith. As you reflect on this incredible brother, missionary, apostle, and martyr, what percentage of his spiritual life would you say was spent in worship to God? How would he answer such a question? Did Paul ever "go to church?" Did he ever attend "services?" Did he think of worship as something he went to for one or two hours a week?

These may seem like strange questions to be asking about Paul. After all, they would be easy for us to answer, so how much easier would it be for a spiritual giant like Paul? They would be difficult questions for Paul because they represent twenty centuries of tradition which have dramatically changed the biblical concepts of "worship" and "church." Through centuries of cathedral thinking and sanctuary mind-sets, we see worship and church as something you "go to" rather than something we are.

Did he really think that everything he did was done in the name of Jesus? Sure, he said in Colossians 3:17 that ". . . whatever you do in word or deed, *do* all in the name of the Lord Jesus." But was he talking about everything we do?

In 1 Corinthians 10:31, after making it clear that we have the right to eat any kind of food but must be considerate of others whose conscience won't let them eat certain things, he declared, "Whether, then, you eat or drink or whatever you do, do all to the glory of God." Was he truly teaching that everything, even mundane things like eating and drinking, should glorify God? Is this something that we do all the time?

What about Paul's multiple use in Ephesians 1 of the phrase "to the praise of His glory" to describe not only what we do, but what we are in response to our redemption by God (vv. 6,12, and 14)? He seems to be clearly saying that we live to praise God.

Obviously, praising and glorifying God are not things that we do for just a short while on Sunday morning. At least Paul never taught that. So — is worship something different than praising and glorifying God, and doing things in His name? They seem to be unlimited and all-inclusive, while we've always thought of worship as limited to a time and place, and exclusive of anything else we might do. After all, you can serve God all week long, but if you miss the Sunday morning assembly you've missed worship — right?

Paul told us very clearly when, where, and how he worshiped God. Paul was the apostle to the Gentiles and it seems that some of the Gentiles, at least some in Rome, were getting a little prideful about it. In chapter 11 of Romans he takes a little of the wind out of their sails when he explains that "God has not rejected His people," the Jews. Then he declares, "May it never be! For I too am an Israelite." He uses several analogies to make the point that Israel is important to God and that they, the Gentiles, are the Johnny-Come-Latelies to the Lord. He said, "Do not be arrogant," verse 18, and then in verse 20, "Do not be conceited, but fear."

He then turns his and the readers' attention to the greatness and power of God. He mentions the kindness and the severity of God, which are both elements of holiness. He declares, "God is able to graft them (Israel) in again." God can do anything. He is incredible, "for the gifts and the calling of God are irrevocable." Paul seems to get caught up in the wonder of God's mercy as he says,

> For God has shut up all in disobedience that He might show mercy to all. Oh, the depth of the riches both of the wisdom and knowledge of God! How unsearchable are His judgments and unfathomable His ways! For who has known the mind of the Lord, or who became His counselor? Or who has first given to Him that it might be paid back to him again? For from Him and through Him and to Him are all things. To Him *be* the glory forever. Amen (vv. 32-36).

Since we have such a wonderful, loving, and gracious God, what should we do to show our gratitude and to praise Him in worship? Paul tells us — no, he pleads with us,

> I urge you therefore, brethren, by the mercies of God, to present your bodies a living and holy sacrifice, acceptable to God, *which* is your spiritual service of worship. And do not be conformed to this world, but be transformed by the renewing of your mind, that you may prove what the will of God is, that which is good and acceptable and perfect (Rom 12:1-2).

While there are scores of other passages that help to define worship in the New Testament, this passage sums up Paul's theology of worship in the New Covenant, and more importantly, what God expects our worship to look like. That is why the context is so important. Paul's plea is based on what God wants our response to Him to be.

OOZING WITH WORSHIP

When something was dominant in a person's character or actions, we used to say that they were "oozing with" it. The young man who is trying to impress a certain girl might be "oozing with sweetness." The husband who is trying to convince his wife that he "NEEDS" to go on that hunting trip to Colorado will be "oozing with kindness." (I know that one first hand.) The little girl with chocolate on her face and crumbs on her dress might be "oozing with guilt" when she's asked about the cookies missing from the cookie jar.

Nearly every word of Paul's plea in Romans 12:1 and 2 is "oozing with" the concept of "total." Total, not as in the cereal Total™ or a mathematical sum, but as in complete, everything, entire, all-inclusive, and "the whole enchilada."

I know — "oozing with total" is a redundancy, but that just enhances the emphasis I want to make. Paul makes it clear that God wants a *total*, all-or-nothing commitment to Him, and that's the only worship that is acceptable.

When we look at this passage word by word and phrase by phrase, God's call for total surrender doesn't just ooze, it pours forth into any heart that will receive it.

"I urge you therefore, brethren, by the mercies of God ..."

All of us preacher-teacher-types, usually zoom through this phrase to hurry on to the "good stuff." But this is the good stuff too! Look at the combination of elements. It includes a personal beseeching, a call for a logical conclusion, a tender touch of family, and a focus on God's grace.

Paul's use of the word "urge" is not insignificant to this study. He didn't say, "I ask you," which clearly carries no authority with it, and yet he didn't say, "I command you," which is authoritative. He used the word *parakaleo*, which is translated "urge" in the NASB, and seems to be somewhere in the middle between "ask" and "command." It's as if he had the right to order this, but he chose a passionate plea instead. He wanted the reader to understand that this was a personal, heart-level plea from him and the Holy Spirit. It's the Greek version of "please." [1]

"Therefore" is the connection with the things mentioned in the preceding chapter. Since God is so amazingly wonderful, and we all agree that "to Him be the glory forever," what is the next logical step? What must we "therefore" do? It is a form of syllogistic reasoning that says:

Major premise: God has given us everything
Minor premise: He deserves everything that we can give to Him
Conclusion or "therefore": We must ...

It is here that their teacher, their missionary, their apostle, and their spiritual father refers to them as "brethren." It is not just a term of endearment, but a term of relationship and equality. He was obviously a leader, but he was also a member of the family of God, an adopted child, saved and humbled by grace. He could have called them "children" or even "sheep" or even "soldiers," whose job it is to carry out orders. Instead, he called them and us family. Again, he purposely chose to ignore authority and speak from compassion, but then that is consistent with "the mercies of God." Paul is displaying what he calls on us to admire most about God.

God is the giver of gifts, the greatest of which is salvation through His Son, Jesus Christ. When Paul gets to this conclusion/therefore part of his message, he provides the reader with all the motivation necessary to heed his plea. We are urged to respond to "the mercies of God," which are rich, unsearchable, and unfathomable (v. 33). The word "mercies" is used not to emphasize the plural nature of His gifts to us, but to show how intense and great His mercy is. It is really the idea of "great mercy" or "great compassion" that He, as Paul says in Ephesians 1:8, "lavished upon us."[2]

Paul has forcefully yet beautifully packaged the Major and Minor Premise of his syllogism so that the want-to-be-worshiper is sitting on the edge of his pew saying "Yes! Yes! Please, just tell me what I need to do to show my love for God! I'll do anything — just tell me what it is!" Then he launched the torpedo that blew all the laws and traditions of man clear out of the water!

"Present your bodies a living and holy sacrifice, acceptable to God . . ."

Few passages declare the change and contrast between the old and new covenants as this one does. Under the Old Law, the worshiper obediently followed the smallest detail of the regulations as to how they were to offer sacrifices to God. They would take their offering, which may have been as big as an ox or as small as a dove, depending on their wealth, to the priest to be offered on their behalf. It was costly, very time consuming, and a total commitment on the part of the animal. This was done at the temple, by the priests, and the people supplied the sacrifice.

What a difference a resurrection can make! In the New Covenant, our bodies are the temple of God (1 Cor 6:19-20), every child of God is a priest (1 Pet 2:9), and Jesus became the "once for all" sacrifice "when He offered up Himself" (Heb 7:27). For us to enjoy all the benefits of that one great sacrifice that Jesus made, we must make a sacrifice ourselves. We offer or present ourselves to God, on His altar of love, and sacrifice ourselves to Him every minute of every hour of every day. It's not a "Sunday thing" any more than it's a "Monday thing." It's a living thing! We do it — it's in effect, as long as we are living. Once we die, we are no longer a living sacrifice but an eternal sacrifice dwelling with God in His holy city.

The totality of our relationship with God is obvious here. Our sacrifice is total. It's even more total than a sacrifice of death. Death is a one-time event. We must *live* for Him *and* be holy for Him. It is only that total sacrifice that is acceptable to God. Many have wanted to keep that sacrifice limited to one hour on Sunday and a contribution check, but that has nothing in common with the truth of what God desires from us.

Can you imagine the Jew bringing his best lamb to the temple to be sacrificed and telling the priest that he only wants to offer a part of the lamb? Maybe the tail or one hoof or an ear? Sacrifice was an all-or-nothing activity, and that principle didn't change with the coming of the New Covenant. Remember the objective. Our heart's desire is to please and be acceptable to God. Paul is spelling out exactly what that is. Anything less than a living and holy sacrifice is no more acceptable to God than Cain's offering was.

I've never cared much about joining the fight over which translation of the Bible is best or most accurate. I just praise God that His Word is being read — whatever version it is. I do take exception with the Revised Standard Version rendition of Romans 12:1 — the one I memorized decades ago. The Greek does not say or intimate "present your bodies as a living sacrifice." The word "as" is not there. Paul is not talking metaphorically. Our bodies must be "a living and holy sacrifice" literally, totally, and really! It is what we *are* not what we are *like*.

When we are a living and holy sacrifice that is acceptable to God, what does He call it?

"*. . . which is your spiritual service of worship.*"

Sacrifice was always part of the Old Covenant worship. It was an act of worship. It was an act of obedience that glorified God. But now God redefines the sacrifice and therefore He redefines worship. Sacrifice is still worship — it's just that the sacrifice is your life. So how does that redefine worship?

William Barclay, in his commentary on Romans, explained the meaning of this verse by paraphrasing Paul. He said,

> So, take your body; take all the tasks that you have to do every day; take the ordinary work of the shop, the factory, the shipyard, the mine; and offer all that as an act of worship to God.

Then he added,

> True worship is the offering to God of one's body, and all that one does every day with it. Real worship is not the offering to God of a liturgy, however noble, and a ritual, however magnificent. Real worship is the offering of everyday life to him, not something transacted in a church, but

23

something which sees the whole world as the temple of the living God . . . . A man may say, "I am going to church to worship God," but he should also be able to say, "I am going to the factory, the shop, the office, the school, the garage, the locomotive shed, the mine, the shipyard, the field, the byre, the garden, to worship God."[3]

Worship that pleases God must be "a living and holy sacrifice" to Him. The traditional concept of worship being something you attend on Sunday did not come from the Bible. It came from man's traditions, from hundreds of years of cathedral focus and centuries of ignoring Scripture. It permeates our vocabulary, our literature, and our thinking. We go to worship — we leave worship, and never realize that we have reduced to an hour what God said must be our *entire* life.

The word for worship in verse one is *latreia*. It is the word that most accurately and consistently describes what God wants us to do to show our love and adoration of Him. The word originally meant "to work for hire or pay." Not in the sense of slavery, but rather the voluntary acceptance of work in return for a salary. It came to mean service, "but it also came to mean *that to which a man gives his whole life*." It was the word that was used to describe a person's service to the gods and the dedication of one's life to that service. Paul chose the word carefully. Our worship is to be as total as our sacrifice. In the five times it's used in the New Testament, it is never used to describe service to humans, and always used in connection to serving and worshiping God.[4]

My first two books on worship dealt extensively with this principle. (See *Spilt Grape Juice* and *Unbroken Bread* from College Press.) I do not plan to rewrite or restate all of that material, but it is significant to note that the word "worship," in whatever Greek word you like best, is never used in the New Testament in connection with a Christian assembly. The problem is that we don't begin with a biblical definition of worship when we study or talk about it. We take our preconceived, preprogrammed conclusions with us into our reading of the Bible and fail to wonder why we see nothing in it that resembles what we do. God wants *latreia*, and all we give Him are a couple of hours of rituals on Sunday!

TOTAL WORSHIP — TOTAL CHANGE!

I received a brochure the other day inviting me to attend a workshop on worship being held at a large, progressive church in our area. This is a congregation that is on the cutting edge of change, innovation, and relevancy. I respect and admire them greatly. Yet, the first line in the description of their worship workshop states, "The primary function of the church is worship." Oh really? I'd love to see some New Testament Scriptures to back that statement up! I guess I would agree with it if they were talking about helping Christians to be living and holy sacrifices for God, but the nuts and bolts of the workshop involve "worship committees, praise teams, and multimedia" being used to create a "healthy worship environment." While I am in favor of all these things, they are talking about the Christian *assembly* not worship.

Worship is a life given in obedience to God. God told us to meet together to encourage, edify, and equip one another; so when we do that, God is obeyed and therefore worshiped, but no more than when we obey Him anywhere else at any other time. The Christian assembly is not THE worship. It may have been called that for the last fifteen centuries, but it was never understood to be that in the first century. If we don't start understanding that our worship to Him is total, we will continue to give Him only part of what He asks for. Again, worship is a "living sacrifice" not two or three hours on Sunday.

Being "a living and holy sacrifice" and offering acceptable worship to God requires a total change in our living
and our thinking. Paul followed up his description of
acceptable worship with "how" and "why" we should do
it. Read it again, but more slowly this time:

> And do not be conformed to this world, but be trans-
> formed by the renewing of your mind, that you may prove
> what the will of God is, that which is good and acceptable
> and perfect (Rom 12:2).

To use my favorite redundancy, this verse is oozing with
totality! There are few words that speak to the essence of
totality as the words transformation and renewal do. It is a
call for us to rise to a new level of spirituality. A level
where we are totally absorbed by our desire to obey and to
please our Father.

This world really gets in the way of things, doesn't it?
Paul is urging us to recognize that the world is a huge barrier on our path to being living sacrifices for God. It lures
us into apathy, tempts us to fulfill fleshly desires, it appeals
to our pride, our need for acceptance and worldly security,
and it subtly molds us into conformity with the rest of
mankind. It's all part of Satan's plan. He's the Prince of this
world and the master deceiver. He can sell forbidden fruit
as brain food and convince people that a life of worship is
really only one hour a week. He doesn't like total worship,
living sacrifices, and being acceptable to God. He's into
straining, limiting, reducing, and minimizing. He wants
Christians to offer their bodies as living sacrifices on the
altar of materialism, egotism, traditionalism, legalism, and
conformity. He'll settle for owning just part of our life,
while God says we're either all His or not His at all!

The transformation that Paul is urging us to be part of is
the change from following the world to being guided by
Jesus. This is a change in the inward person, the spirit, the
personality, the part of man that is touched by the indwelling

of Jesus Christ. We are no longer "dominated by human nature" but "the essential man has been changed; now he lives, not a self-centered but a Christ-centered life."[5]

The present tense of "renewing of your mind" means that this is an ongoing activity for Christians. The Spirit wants us to regularly reflect on the commitment we made to God and reaffirm it over and over again. In doing this, we stay connected to God's will. When we stay tuned in to His will, we do three things. First, we stay focused on what is good. Second, we are doing what pleases (acceptable) God. And finally, we make sure that we don't leave out something that's part of the complete (or perfect) will of God.[6] It's important to note that being "a living and holy sacrifice" and the "renewing of your mind" are both total, ongoing, and pleasing/acceptable to God.

I love Barclay's summation comment on these two verses. He said, "When Christ becomes the center of life then we can present real worship, which is the offering of every moment and every action to God."[7]

God, the Holy Spirit, Paul, and all the Christians in New Testament times had a much different definition of worship than what we traditionally have today. In previous books, I have defined worship as a life given in obedience to God. After restudying Romans 12:1-2 again and seeing how complete, how total, and how never-ending our worship is (or should be), I feel a need for a more accurate and inclusive definition. Is there something in the New Testament that includes all of these elements and gives us a much more complete definition of Christian worship? Is there a concept talked about in Scripture that fits William Barclay's description of "real worship, which is the offering of every moment and every action to God"?

Obviously, I think there is or I wouldn't be writing this book. Now that we have the concept of "total" worship introduced, let's put the pieces together and see what they build.

DISCUSSION QUESTIONS

1. If Paul were asked about how often he "worshiped," what do you think his answer would be?

2. Is it more difficult for modern man to understand the full meaning of "living sacrifice" than it was for those in New Testament times? Why?

3. What are some words or concepts in the Bible that require our total focus and life?

4. Why is it so difficult for us to stop thinking of worship as something we "go to" as opposed to what "we are"?

CHAPTER TWO
Stewards of a Promise

If you had to be baptized in a Rocky Mountain natural spring, you would either have a stronger argument for sprinkling or an incredible test of faith. I've been in a Colorado stream, at ten thousand feet elevation, just feet from where the water poured from its underground refrigerator, and there was nothing fun or enjoyable about it. I know, telling a story about "how cold the water was" is like telling about pain, scars, or how hard you worked — everyone can top your story. Unless you've been to the Antarctic, cut a hole in the glacial ice and jumped in, I don't want to hear about it!

The first time I decided to bathe in that mountain stream, it was after several hours of hunting and hiking. The terrain was rugged and challenging, and the air was quite thin, so I was worn-out and very hot. I waited until midafternoon, when the sun was at its peak and the temperature was the highest in hopes that it would take the edge off the cold water. It didn't. It was so cold that it was instantly painful to the touch. I knew that I would have to do my bathing quickly, totally, and courageously. With shorts and tennis shoes on, I launched into the one-foot deep water, sat down, leaned back, and came up scrubbing. I also came up gasping for air and shaking the mountains with a feral yell of pain. I shivered so violently that I couldn't hold on to my soap and shampoo bottle. After I savagely lathered up my body, I rebaptized myself and came up, I'm sure, with no living germ or speck of dirt on my body. I was as purple as a plum and shaking like an aspen leaf in a hurricane.

I'd been swimming in cold water in many other places, but I'd never before been in water that was so cold it felt like it was burning. My commitment to bathing became much less total. I learned the value of a good washcloth bath. It wasn't as thorough as a bath, but it was a lot less painful. Besides, after the shock of that first attempt wore off and sensation returned to my body, it really wasn't that difficult to put up with a little bit of uncleanliness.

ALL OR NOTHIN'

When I took that plunge into that Colorado stream, every fiber of my body screamed, "Get me out of here!" Jesus knew exactly what was going to happen to Him. There wasn't anything that He didn't know if He chose to know it. Plus, crucifixions were a regular occurrence in His day and time. He knew precisely how horribly painful that Roman practice was. He was flesh and blood, and every fiber of His body was saying to His Father, "Please — get me out of here!" His actual request, as you remember, was, "My Father, if it is possible, let this cup pass from Me; yet not as I will, but as Thou wilt" (Matt 26:39,42, and 44).

It wasn't that He didn't want to wash away our sins,

redeem us, and reconcile us to God. He knew before the creation of the world that His sacrifice would be necessary in order for us to have hope. It was just a matter of grappling with the physical aspects of the sacrifice. He didn't have the luxury of giving a partial sacrifice, a little sacrifice, or an almost sacrifice. He had to give a total sacrifice. He and God couldn't put up with "a little bit of uncleanliness." The cleansing power of His blood was in His total gift of love, His total submission to the will of His Father, and the total offering of His life.

When Paul declared that acceptable worship involved our being a "living sacrifice" for God, He was describing a sacrifice that was as total as the one Jesus offered for us. Jesus gave Himself totally to the will of God. He was crucified, giving everything for us, and He was raised from the dead and "is able to do exceeding abundantly beyond all that we ask or think, according to the power that works within us" (Eph 3:20).

As we put the pieces together to develop a new, more biblically accurate definition of worship, we must understand that this principle is one of the most vital parts. *Our whole life is worship because worship is being a total and constant living sacrifice.* Just in case you missed the importance of connecting our "living sacrifice" with Jesus' "dying sacrifice," listen to another one of Paul's "totality" passages.

> I have been crucified with Christ; and it is no longer I who live, but Christ lives in me; and the *life* which I now live in the flesh I live by faith in the Son of God, who loved me, and delivered Himself up for me (Gal 2:20).

There's a lot of "oozing" going on in that passage. How total is our crucifixion with Christ supposed to be? How totally does Christ live in us? How totally are we to live by faith? Just as total as Jesus' sacrifice and our living sacrifice, and just as total as our worship.

31

TOTALLY THERE!

Contrary to what we may sound like, we preacher-types really don't know everything. That is one of the reasons why I don't mind hanging out my dirty laundry for everyone to see when I preach or write. I like for people to know that I've learned a lot of lessons the hard way and I continue to do dumb things every now and then. Everyone, but especially ministers, must never stop learning and growing. One of the greatest sources of learning for me is my brethren. I have been blessed to be able to have plenty of conscientious and dedicated people in my congregation who teach and inspire me. Tim is one such person.

Not long ago, Tim was telling me about a very successful seminar and meeting that he directed out of state for the advertising company he worked for. At the end of the meeting, after everyone left, he found himself cleaning, wiping tables, and moving furniture. He said that he caught himself thinking, "Hey, I was the featured speaker at this thing. I shouldn't have to clean tables." He quickly realized that wasn't the kind of thinking a child of God should have. What came to his mind next was what it meant to be a "living sacrifice" for God. He remembered that the Old Testament sacrifices were offered on the altar before God, and the altar represented the presence of God. "If we are living sacrifices," he said, "constantly being offered on the altar before God, then whatever I do and wherever I go, I am in the presence of God!" His smile and bright eyes showed me that this was an exciting revelation for him. He said, "All of a sudden, I was wiping tables in the presence of God! Everything I was — everything I did — needed to be done in such a way that it was acceptable to Him! How could I ever be grumpy while in the presence of God!"

Wow — what a concept! How would it change our lives if we maintained a constant awareness of the presence of God? After all, when is He not present? As Paul told the crowd on Mars Hill in Acts 17, "He is not far from each one of us; for in Him we live and move and exist" (vv. 27-28).

Since we live, move, and exist in the presence of God, shouldn't everything we do, say, or think be acceptable to Him? We've been taught that our singing must be done from the heart and acceptable to God, but what about the way I drive my car? We know that the Lord's Supper, the *koinonia* feast, must be taken in "a worthy manner," but what about when I gather with my family to eat my supper, which He gave me? Obviously my contribution to the church must be liberal, cheerful, and grateful, but what about the rest of my money? Do I have to use it in such a way that it's acceptable to God? When am I free to ignore what God wants?

If you think you have to go to church on Sunday morning to "encounter God," be "in His presence," or "worship Him," then you obviously believe there are times when you don't have to be concerned with pleasing Him. You won't find any place in the New Testament where these ideas of a special presence or encounter with God are part of the Christian assembly. Someone might ask, "Aren't we in the presence of God during our times together and shouldn't we rejoice over it?" Of course, but only because we know He is always with us. There is no more a special presence of God on Sunday morning at the church building than there is in your car Monday morning, or in your office Monday afternoon, or with your family around the dinner table, or when you are alone in your thoughts and prayers while laying in bed that night.

The idea of a limited or special presence of God comes from temple traditions and cathedral thinking. It causes us to reduce God to a time and place, minimize our responsibility to be aware of Him, and turns our spiritual walk into a once-a-week stroll with the Father.

So the next piece in building a new and more accurate definition of worship is to understand that *our whole life is worship because worship is an awareness of the presence of God and it's something we always do.*

We don't know who wrote the Epistle of Hebrews, but whoever he was, he sure knew a lot about the Old Law and Temple worship. (Sounds an awful lot like Paul to me!) His theme throughout the entire epistle seems to be that everything is "better" in the New Covenant, so why even think about wanting to go back to the Mosaic Covenant. Towards the end of the epistle, in chapter 12, he makes several more arguments about how much better off we are now as part of His church, the kingdom. In view of how wonderful it is to be part of His kingdom, we should do something for God in response to His love. He said,

> Therefore, since we receive a kingdom which cannot be shaken, let us show gratitude, by which we may offer to God an acceptable service with reverence and awe (Heb 12:28).

It is very important that we first notice that what God wants from us must come from a sense of gratitude. After much study and prayer, I am convinced that gratitude or thankfulness is the foundation of every spiritual quality that God wants us to have. Just think about it. What spiritual quality can you have and develop without first having a grateful spirit? Humility? Love? Patience? Unselfishness? Check out the Christian Graces in 2 Peter 1 or the fruit of the Spirit in Galatians 5, and see if any of them can be a major part of our life without gratefulness. In fact, most of them will not make sense to us unless we understand gratefulness.

Because we are grateful to be part of a kingdom that is unshakable and eternal, we need to offer to God only what is acceptable to Him. What does He want us to do in response to our gratefulness? How do we show gratitude to God? We serve with reverence and awe!

The word for "serve" is a form of the Greek word *latreuo (latreuomen)*, which we've already examined, and it is translated as either "worship" or "service." Most translations and commentaries use the word "service" because "worship may be too narrow . . . for the word can be used of service of various kinds."[8] That is exactly right if you use a traditional definition of worship. The Hebrew writer is clearly talking about us offering to God something more than attending "Worship" once a week — two or three times if you're really spiritual.

The problem with that line of logic is that the Hebrew writer knew nothing about "going to church," or "going to worship services!" There was no such thing in New Testament times as "formal worship" and "informal worship." There were no church buildings, no set patterns for opening and closing prayers, invitation songs, worship leaders, worship schedules, Sunday-go-to-meetin' clothes, calls to worship, devotionals, sacraments, sanctuaries, communion tables, pulpits, pews, and while I can't prove it as I can these others, I just know there weren't any closing announcements.

The bottom line is the Hebrew writer had absolutely no reason to see the word "worship" as being limiting or narrow. In the New Testament, worship is as broad and unlimited as service. Worship is only restricted by our traditional thinking about worship, and that tradition comes from many centuries of cathedral-thinking domination and influence.

A grateful heart is constantly aware of God's presence and God's goodness. It compels that person to serve God by serving others, just as we love God by loving others. This never-ending offering is never done grudgingly or half-heartedly, but rather with "reverence and awe." What does that mean? It only has meaning if you understand the constant presence of God. He is the only one worthy of reverence and awe! That is why we do everything in "the name of Jesus" and "to the glory of God" (Col 3:17 and 1 Cor 10:31). Everything! Our lives must totally reflect the presence of God!

I think it is amazing and ironic that reverence for God is never described in the New Testament as an attitude we must have inside a building, but a respect we show for Him by doing His will. The solemn expression, the sacred atmosphere, the dramatic background music, the rituals, the robes, the whispers, and the feel of holiness − may seem like reverence, but you won't find it in the New Testament.

Real reverence − real worship − is constantly being aware of the presence of God.

CROSS MY HEART AND HOPE TO DIE

Remember all the things you used to go through when you were a kid to make sure that a friend was telling you the truth? We used to go through a series of questions that made a swearing in in a courtroom look inconsequential. Once the secret or the information had been given, we always began with, "Are you sure?" Then it went to the next level of commitment and sincerity with the question, "Do you promise?" Once that was passed, the next challenge was, "Cross you heart and hope to die?" They couldn't just say "yes" to this. They had to literally and physically cross their heart with their hand. The only thing left to do after that was to check fingers, arms, legs, toes, and even eyes, and make sure nothing was crossed. A crossed anything negated the promise. Many compromising situations were avoided through the adroit use of crossed fingers, or some other body parts.

I remember it like it was yesterday. I was in elementary school in my home town of Washington, D.C. Right after saying our prayer, pledge to the flag, and taking attendance, the teacher said she had an important announcement for us. We sat there spellbound. She'd never done anything like this before. She said, "As you know from our

Current Events, President Eisenhower has been in a very important meeting with the Russian leaders. He really did a wonderful job and got some things started that will limit future nuclear weapons escalation . Well, his plane is landing at Bowling Air Force Base at 10 o'clock this morning, and it has been decided that all the Public Schools will dismiss classes for the day so that we can all be there to cheer him when he gets off the plane."

We screamed with delight! Alright — a day off from school! Some kids actually headed for their in-room lockers to start putting away their books and supplies. Then she started laughing. I instantly knew that something wasn't right. There was just something sinister about the tone of her laughter.

As everyone froze in various stages of jubilation, she yelled, "April fools!" It was then that I remembered it was April 1st. I was crushed. I can take a joke about a lot of things, but getting out of school was not one of them. Getting out of school was always serious business.

I wonder if anyone standing before God on the Day of Judgment will say, "God, I had my fingers crossed when I promised to live for you. So my promise doesn't count." Would someone dare to dodge their accountability to God for lying when they confessed Jesus as their Lord and Savior by saying, "It was April fools!"

It would be just as bad to tell God, "I know I promised to be a living sacrifice, but I decided that one hour on Sunday was sufficient." How about saying, "God, I know that I was in your presence all the time, but I chose to recognize your presence only when I walked into the church building and attended the formal worship."

Before weak excuses like that are made to God, we need to remember what the Holy Spirit said to any Christian who "has trampled under foot the Son of God, and has regarded as unclean the blood of the covenant by which he was sanctified, and has insulted the Spirit of grace." He pointed

37

out that it was God who said, "Vengeance is Mine, I will repay," and "The Lord will judge His people." Then He lowered the boom on those who take lightly their commitment to God. He declared, "It is a terrifying thing to fall into the hands of the living God" (Heb 10:29-31).

God keeps His promises to us, and He expects us to keep our promises to Him. So any new and more biblically accurate definition of worship must recognize that *worship involves our total life because worship is a promise we made and continually reaffirm to God*. No one forced us to present our bodies to God as living sacrifices. That was a choice, a commitment, and a promise we made in response to our merciful God. He said that He would redeem us and "bless us with every spiritual blessing in the heavenly *places* in Christ," if we would promise to "be holy and blameless before Him," (Eph. 1:3-4) which is the same thing as being a "living and holy sacrifice." In the Bible, this kind of offer, deal, or agreement is called a covenant.

This could be an incredible life-changing concept if you will chew on it awhile. *Worship is a covenant between God and us.* While the concept of covenant is primarily the making of a promise, for those of us who walk through the sacred pages it carries connotations of spiritual connections, biblical history, and timeless dependability. Our promise to live for Jesus is no less important and binding than promises made by Abraham and David. A covenant is a reciprocal agreement with the living God, who gave a living sacrifice and asked us to be living sacrifices in return. If we keep our part of the covenant, He will allow us to dwell in eternity with Him, in a special place He's prepared just for us.

The most amazing part of the covenant is His grace. He constantly forgives our sins, mistakes, weaknesses, and shortcomings, as long as we continue to walk in the light, with our focus on Jesus (1 John 1:7). In essence, even though we can't keep the covenant perfectly, He'll keep it intact as long as we keep the spirit of it.

What He wants from us as our part of the covenant is a life offered up in continual worship to Him. Anything less than total living worship is a violation of our covenant with God. We can't choose to reduce it, shrink it, limit it, minimize it, institutionalize it, or traditionalize it. God's grace is greater than we will ever know, but reducing what is supposed to be total living down to one or two hours on Sunday may be stretching its limits.

Another way to think about worship as a covenant is to look at what it means to be Christlike. When are we supposed to be Christlike? Which day of the week or hour of the day do we put on our be-like-Jesus outfits and try to imitate Him? You're saying, "That's insane," because you know that we "put on Christ" are "crucified with Christ" and, like Paul, should be able to say, "For me to live is Christ." We are always Christlike! Our goal is to mature spiritually, which means that we want to grow "to the measure of the stature which belongs to the fullness of Christ." We "grow up in all *aspects* into Him, who is the head, *even* Christ" (Eph 4:13,15).

Being like Jesus is our part of the covenant with God. Being like Jesus is what it means to be "a living and holy sacrifice" which is worship that pleases God. Isn't it accurate then to say that if *worship is a covenant, and our covenant is to be Christlike, then worship is being Christlike*? If our life is worship and our life is to be Christlike, it seems logical to me that when you and I are being like Jesus we are worshiping God. Isn't that what is being said in Hebrews 13:15-16? See if you don't see all these parts of our covenant with God in this passage.

> Through Him then, let us continually offer up a sacrifice of praise to God, that is, the fruit of lips that give thanks to His name. And do not neglect doing good and sharing; for with such sacrifices God is pleased.

No one, not even hard-core traditionalists, would argue against the conclusion that the goal of worship is to please God. Okay, according to this passage, what pleases God? (Remember, two chapters earlier, in 11:6, the writer said that faith pleased God, so this too must all be part of the faith God wants.) First, it happens through Jesus. In Him, because of Him, and through Him, we do everything we do. The phrase "Through Him then" is just another way of saying "in your efforts to be Christlike." The goal of worship then is for everything to be Christ centered.

Secondly, "we must offer up a sacrifice of praise to God," and the Holy Spirit is very precise about when: continually! Exactly which day of the week is that? Is that morning or evening services? Continually means nonstop! Whatever the sacrifice is and whatever the praise is, it never ends! This is a powerful message about the totality of worship. We offer a sacrifice of praise wherever we are and with whomever we happen to be. Sacrifice is not just going to church on Sunday morning, and praise is not just singing "Hallelujah, Praise Jehovah." It is what we *are* as Christians.

Thirdly, just look at the description of what sacrifice and praise to God are. They are "the fruit" or results, of "lips that give thanks to His name." When are we supposed to be thankful? Always! (1 Thess 5:18). Open up your concordance or pull up on your computer the word "thanks" and all the other forms of the word and see how all-inclusive and encompassing it is in our life as Christians. It's what we are — grateful, thankful children! When we live and speak thankfully, the results are continual offerings for God.

Finally, the writer amplifies his definition of sacrifices by describing them as "doing good and sharing." These things please God. What are they? Serving! When do we do them? Well, we've always said we go to "services" so maybe that's what he's talking about? Not! For it to be pleasing to

God it has to be a sacrifice, and the only sacrifice He wants is "a living and holy sacrifice." He wants Christlike living, which is thankful, praising, fruit producing, sacrificial, and total. That's commitment, that's a covenant, and that's real worship!

THE WHOLE PACKAGE

Maybe it's been overkill, but we've looked at worship from several different angles to make sure we understand that worship is our total life given to God. The totality of worship is seen *in our living sacrifice, in the awareness of God's presence, in being Christlike, and in recognizing worship as a covenant with God.*

Is there a concept or spiritual principle that embodies all of these elements? Is there something that gives us that new and more accurate definition of worship we've been studying about? Will it be consistent and true to the New Testament teaching on worship? Can it meet all of the criteria for totality?

Actually, all these elements are found in some very familiar words. Would it not be accurate and biblical to say that worship is faithfulness? Faithfulness is total. For that matter, so is holiness. Isn't worship being holy? These, and other terms, are good and correct, but they bring so much theological baggage with them that it's almost impossible for us to identify with them. Being holy just seems too out of reach, though by God's grace it certainly isn't. Faithfulness, while beautiful and always applicable, has too much controversy and theological history to be a NEW definition for worship. While there aren't and never were "Five Acts of Worship" in the New Testament (rather only one — faithfulness), it doesn't give us the sense of totality that we need.

The most descriptive, complete, accurate, and biblical definition of worship is found in *stewardship. Everything*

God wants and expects from us, in terms of worship, is found in the New Testament concept of stewardship. All the things in the New Testament that define a good steward and describe the elements of spiritual stewardship, also give us a new and accurate definition for worship.

We are stewards of God. We don't go do "steward" things at a special time for stewardship — it's what we are! Stewardship is being responsible for something that was given to us. What are we *not* stewards of? Everything we are and have is a gift from God and we must be responsible for all of it. Since we will be held accountable for what has been given, we must make sure that it reflects positively on the One who gave it. It must glorify Him! Everything — every day! Just like worship! Consider the similarities.

Can we be "a living and holy sacrifice" without being a good steward? The whole essence of being a living sacrifice is our giving back what has been given to us and attempting to please God. We are the stewards and God is the Master, so we are in the business of doing what is "acceptable" to Him. A living and holy sacrifice is what He wants; stewardship makes sure that that is what He receives. They are virtually the same thing.

Can we be good stewards if we aren't constantly and totally aware of the presence of God? It's because we know He's always there that we never stop wanting to please Him.

If worship is being like Jesus, and it is, was there ever a time when Jesus wasn't a good steward? He set the example for stewardship. He lived to please His Father and His Master. If we are going to be like Him we must be totally dedicated stewards.

Worship is our promise, or covenant, to live completely for God. Our lives will praise and glorify Him wherever we are and whatever we do. Isn't that being a good steward? Stewardship is the ongoing fulfillment of our covenant with God. To the extent that we are faithful stewards, to that extent God is worshiped.

Stewardship is total Christian living, which is exactly what worship is. Stewardship and worship aren't places, things, and times. On the contrary, they both define our life. They describe what pleases God. They aren't the checklist checking, ticket punching, ritualistic, Sunday morning religion that tradition says they are.

When Paul was reaching the end of his life, he described his life as "being poured out like a drink offering." He never understood his responsibility to God as anything less than a total living sacrifice. As he wrote about his life ending he said, "I have fought the good fight, I have finished the course, I have kept the faith." Wasn't he telling us that he had been a good steward of all the gifts, responsibilities, and talents that God had given him. He didn't have to mention "going to church" or how many "worships" he'd attended because his life had been offered to God as acceptable worship. As a result, he could confidently say, "In the future there is laid up for me the crown of righteousness, which the Lord, the righteous Judge, will award to me on that day" (2 Tim 4:6-8).

DISCUSSION QUESTIONS

1. Why is it important for us to remember that we are always in the presence of God? How does it change things?

2. Where did the idea of being "reverent" in the church building come from? What do you think about it?

3. What do you think about defining worship as "keeping and reaffirming the promises we made to God?"

4. How would you define New Testament stewardship?

5. Is stewardship synonymous with New Testament worship? Why or why not?

CHAPTER THREE
Stewards of Gifts

They edited it, cleaned it up, and put it on TV the other night, and it had some of the best special effects ever put into a movie. I'm talking about "Terminator 2," the futuristic Arnold Schwarzenegger action movie that swept the country several years ago. He played the part of a robot from the future. He was sent back in time to save a boy, who would one day become an important leader, from another more sophisticated robot that had been sent back to kill the boy. The "bad guy" robot was a T1000 made out of some kind of liquid metal that allowed it to change itself into any form or likeness it wanted.

The most memorable scene for me took place when the T1000, while chasing the good guys, crashed a truck that was filled with liquid nitrogen. As he attempted to walk away from the wreck, he began to freeze solid because of the liquid nitrogen. Because he was programmed to stay focused on his assignment, he refused to stop even though his feet were frozen to the ground. I can still see the scene of his legs snapping off below the knees as he tried to keep moving. He eventually froze solid and was forced to stop — temporarily of course.

That picture of him losing his legs has burned its image into my memory. If you can picture it (or remember it), let's use that image to help make an important point. What if you lost things for which you were not thankful — things you've ignored, taken for granted, or just plain didn't appreciate like you should? What if they just started disappearing?

Can you imagine losing your feet, legs, and the ability to walk? What about losing the ability to see, hear, taste, touch, and smell? What if the next time you complained about that "old piece of junk" you had to drive, it just vanished, and now you had to walk (assuming you still had your legs, of course)? What if the next time you moaned, "I've got nothing to wear," your closet suddenly became empty and you really did have nothing to wear? Are you ready to live on the street when that "run-down, too small house" you live in disappears?

Take that same idea and apply it to your family. What if you suddenly lost family members for whom you failed to be thankful? Are you thankful for your friends? Do you have to lose them before you realize how special they are? Suppose you lost your country? Are you thankful for your soul?

What's the point? We respond to God in direct proportion to the sense of gratitude we have for what He has done for us. If we don't have a well-developed sense of gratitude for God and what He has done for us, we will have neither the will nor the desire to be "a living and holy sacrifice" offered as worship to Him.

I know that "The fear of the Lord is the beginning of knowledge" (Prov 1:7), but that is just that — the starting point. No one, including God, wants a relationship totally based on fear. He wants the fear to be replaced by love

46

(1 John 4:18). Love and obedience have their foundation in gratitude. From "In the beginning God created the heavens and the earth" (Gen 1:1) to "while we were yet sinners, Christ died for us" (Rom 5:8) and to "Be faithful until death, and I will give you the crown of life" (Rev 2:10), God has blessed us with incredible blessings. We should be so overwhelmed by His loving kindness that we feel compelled to worship Him with all we are and all we have.

That's the point! *All we are and all we have are gifts from God!* Our response to God's gifts is stewardship. Nevertheless, stewardship without gratefulness is just mechanical legalism that means nothing to God. In the Old Covenant He said,

> I hate, I reject your festivals,
> Nor do I delight in your solemn assemblies.
> Even though you offer up to Me burnt offerings and your
>   grain offerings,
> I will not accept *them;*
> And I will not *even* look at the peace offerings of your
>   fatlings.
> Take away from Me the noise of your songs;
> I will not even listen to the sound of your harps.
> But let justice roll down like waters
> And righteousness like an ever-flowing stream (Amos 5:21-24).

God wanted righteousness not rituals. He wanted substance and heart-level godliness that showed itself by consistent living. In the New Covenant He said,

> If I speak with the tongues of men and of angels, but do not have love, I have become a noisy gong or a clanging cymbal. And if I have *the gift of* prophecy, and know all mysteries and all knowledge; and if I have all faith, so as to remove mountains, but do not have love, I am nothing. And if I give all my possessions to feed *the poor,* and if I deliver my body to be burned, but do not have love, it profits me nothing (1 Cor 13:1-3).

God clearly wants our heart to be behind everything we do. A good steward isn't a good steward just because he does good steward things. A good steward must be guided by love. All the things mentioned in this familiar passage are acts of obedience, which would make them acts of worship, and therefore — acts of stewardship. Whatever you want to call it, love must be the reason for it. Love wells up from a heart that is overflowing with gratitude. We can never be good stewards or understand stewardship without having a loving and grateful heart.

Stewardship is the offering of worship we make to God because of the love and goodness He has shown to us. *Stewardship (or worship) is devoting ones life to using every gift that He has given us, to glorify Him.*

We need to define some of those terms before we examine some specifics of stewardship. In the next chapter, we will explore what it means "to glorify Him," but let's first look at some "no-brainer" words. They may be a lot more complicated than you would think.

GIFTS

Few words conjure up positive images like the word "gifts." It immediately makes us think of birthdays, Christmas, anniversaries, and other special occasions when love and appreciation are shown. Some of our best memories are from giving and receiving gifts to and from loved ones. It would be so easy to take a trip down Memory Lane and share with you some of the incredible gifts that have been part of my life — both given and received. But, we're not talking about just any gift now. We're looking at gifts that come from God.

Where do we start? God gave us the world and everything that is in it! He gave us life! The greatest gift came wrapped in swaddling clothes and left in radiant robes, and He has a new set reserved for us! Just look at some of the gifts from God that are specifically mentioned in the New Testament.

"the gift of the Holy Spirit" (Acts 2:38).

"the free gift of God is eternal life in Christ Jesus our Lord" (Rom 6:23).

"Thanks be to God for His indescribable gift!" (1 Cor 9:15).

"For by grace you have been saved . . . it is the gift of God" (Eph 2:8).

"grace was given according to the measure of Christ's gift" (Eph 4:7).

"Do not neglect the spiritual gift within you . . . ." (1 Tim 4:14).

"Those . . . who have tasted of the heavenly gift and have been made partakers of the Holy Spirit" (Heb 6:4).

"Every good thing bestowed and every perfect gift is from above, coming down from the Father . . . ." (Jas 1:17).

". . . for the gifts and the calling of God are irrevocable" (Rom 11:29).

"And since we have gifts that differ according to the grace given to us, let us use them accordingly" (Rom 12:6).

"Now concerning spiritual gifts, brethren, I do not want you to be unaware" (1 Cor 12:1).

"But earnestly desire the greater gifts . . . . Love never fails" (1 Cor 12:31 and 13:8).

That is just a small sample of what is in the Bible. It's pretty impressive, isn't it? God is an amazing giver of gifts. The above verses are primarily dealing with spiritual gifts and say almost nothing about our material blessings. That would be another incredible list! Of course the spiritual blessings are the most important. They deal with our souls, eternity, and heaven. I love Paul's introductory comments in Ephesians when he said,

Blessed *be* the God and Father of our Lord Jesus Christ, who has blessed us with every spiritual blessing in the heavenly places in Christ . . . . In Him we have redemption through His blood, the forgiveness of our trespasses, according to the riches of His grace, which He lavished upon us (1:3,7-8).

God has showered us with spiritual blessings, or as Paul said, "he lavished upon us." He didn't hold anything back. As Peter declared, he "granted to us everything pertaining to life and godliness" (2 Pet 1:3). All things spiritual and all things physical are given to us from God. While the Bible uses the word "gift" in connection with special powers given by the Holy Spirit, and to describe talents that we may have been given, the word is truly more all-inclusive than that. Gifts are every blessing given to us by God. It's that simple, yet that complex!

Maybe it's just the fact that I'm getting older, but I've come to realize how insensitive and ungrateful I have been for most of my life. God has taken such good care of me and granted me so many incredible gifts, that for most of my life I've just assumed that it would always be that way. Right now I am probably more aware of what I have to be thankful for than at any other time in my life. A lot of it has to do with my three children growing up and leaving home. I could fill pages with their accomplishments, things they have done just since they went away to college, but that's not really what I'm talking about.

I look at my three children (and new son-in-law), and I am in awe that God has blessed them so much. They are very talented and intelligent (I know, like their mother), but what about their near perfect health? How do we all deserve that? And most important of all, they each have a love for God that far exceeds what I had at their age. I can't tell you how incredible it is to just sit and listen to them talk about their walk with God, their prayer life, and their desire to do His will. There is nothing better in the whole wide world! It's humbling! It's scary — because I don't deserve it — I can't take credit for it — I never knew how amazing it was going to be! God just decided to bless us with this incomparable blessing!

This says something very important to me. *Spiritual maturity is an awareness and sensitivity to all that God has given us.* It is something that we have to learn. It's a process, like all kinds of maturity.

Babies don't understand the principle of giving and receiving gifts. They want food — now! They want attention — now! They want the discomfort of a wet diaper corrected — now! They don't care about anything else around them. They are the center of the universe and everyone exists to take care of their needs. As they grow, they learn that not everyone has to give them gifts, and they learn how much others enjoy getting gifts from them. Then they spend the rest of their life trying to decide how much of a giver or receiver they should be. It all depends on the level of selfishness they have in their hearts at any given time.

As our relationship with God grows, we come to understand that "Every good thing bestowed and every perfect gift is from above, coming down from the Father of lights, with whom there is no variation, or shifting shadow" (Jas 1:17). Our attitude of gratitude grows. We're not just lucky — we're blessed! We're not just somewhat blessed, but incredibly blessed! As our spirits are broken and our hearts are humbled, we realize that we haven't deserved a single breath of air that we've taken. It's all a gift from God, and we need to live as if it were a treasure to be appreciated — not a right to be expected! And when those tough times come, and they will, we are thankful for what we've had rather than resentful for what we're missing.

It is only when, in a spirit of gratitude, we understand that body, breath, loved ones, and salvation are all undeserved gifts from God that we are truly set free. Free from worry, from loss, and free from the "sting of death."

At the time of this writing, I am forty-eight years old. If God doesn't give me another day to live for Him, how can I feel cheated? I've been given forty eight years of enormous blessings. I've lived longer than the average age of all who have ever lived! I've lived nearly two and a-half times as long as the average age of the fifty-eight thousand fellow Americans who died in Vietnam! I've lived to see my children love and live for God, and I've shared twenty-seven of those forty-eight years with the most incredible Christian woman I've ever known. I've spent over a quarter of a century in full-time ministry for God, and it's been a blessing in nearly every way. I've never struggled with illness and only had very few injuries. Cheated? Robbed? I cannot disrespect God's marvelous gifts by crying, "Give me more!" Every hour He gives me is, as the old farmer said, "nothing but gravy."

OUR

It's a little word, but a very important word. When we talk about "using *our* gifts to glorify God" we must redefine this plural possessive. "Our" is a relative term. Most of the time, when we say "our," we are referring to something "we" share or own.

When we stop talking about what God wants and what His Word says, we seem to degenerate into childlike selfishness again. When we become convicted that our lives are living worship to God, and start asking questions like:

"What does God want us to do and be as a church?"

"What's our purpose?"

"How can we reach our community with the saving message of Jesus?"

"What is the best way to make sure our assemblies glorify God?" — then spiritual maturity will return to "our" churches, along with peace and love.

That is what I mean when I say that "our" is a relative

term. One very familiar introduction changes everything. "In the beginning God created . . ." makes it clear who owns it all. We own nothing — God owns everything! Nothing is really "ours" because it all is really His. He's just lending things to us. It's His stuff and we're just caretakers, laborers, borrowers, servants, custodians, and stewards. We don't really have possessions, we have responsibilities.

What's "our" job? Make sure that every single thing on loan to us from God glorifies Him! That is real worship. How do we do that? Be like Jesus,

> . . . who, although He existed in the form of God, did not regard equality with God a thing to be grasped, but emptied Himself, taking the form of a bond-servant, and being made in the likeness of men. And being found in appearance as a man, He humbled Himself by becoming obedient to the point of death, even death on a cross (Phil 2:6-8).

In Christ, "our" thinking becomes *His* thinking. There are several keys to spiritual "our" thinking in this wonderful passage of Scripture. Jesus "emptied Himself" and thus explained to us the essence of unselfishness. He became "a bond-servant" which means that He didn't belong to Himself, but to God. He showed us that true obedience begins with humility.

It is only when we are humble that God can truly use us and work through us. He "is opposed to the proud, but gives grace to the humble" (Jas 4:6). Too many times we think that acts of obedience are our major focus in our personal life and our congregational life, but Jesus shows that obedience must issue from a humble servant attitude. It's impossible to be Christlike without humility. Maybe that's why so many see no inconsistency in being un-Christlike as they seek to get "their way" in the assembly. Jesus was humble to the point of total sacrifice. He gave Himself completely to the will of God, and this was fully expressed in His death for us.

53

When "our" starts meaning "His" in our life, it will have its fullest expression in our sacrificial service for others. We've got to make that transformation from being full of ourselves to *emptying* ourselves — like Jesus did.

ALL

It's an even smaller word in the phrase "all our gifts," but it needs a special emphasis. At the risk of sounding redundant, we have to deal with the spiritual reality that *"all" means "all."* There is nothing in our life that is exempt from the responsibility to be used to glorify God. I bring to your attention again that startling and challenging charge that Paul gave in 1 Corinthians 10:31, "Whether, then, you eat or drink or whatever you do, do all to the glory of God."

I love the beauty of that passage. How can something as mundane as eating and drinking be done to the glory of God? Does He want us to eat and drink? Absolutely! (This is not a scriptural rationale for gluttony, by the way.) When we do anything that God intended for us to do, it glorifies Him. Remember, worship is obedience and obedience is using whatever God has given us to please Him. That is also what stewardship is all about. It's the commitment to making sure that everything we do glorifies God. Even the little things, the seemingly insignificant things, and the things we ignore or take for granted. Again — *all means all.*

Here's a question that may help put this in perspective. What is beautiful to God? You know what you think is beautiful, but what does He think is beautiful? As my kids would say, "That's a toughie!" You know it's not riches, buildings, jewels, and other material things, because of what Jesus said about the lilies of the field. They had more glory in them than Solomon did as the wealthiest monarch in Jewish history (Matt 6:28-29).

Likewise, God is not very impressed with the wise, the mighty, and the noble, because "God has chosen the foolish things of the world to shame the wise, and God has chosen the weak things of the world to shame the things which are strong, and the base things of the world and the despised, God has chosen, the things that are not, that He might nullify the things that are, that no man should boast before God" (1 Cor 1:26-29). God doesn't care about "all that glitters." God seems to notice things that man ignores – at least ungodly men. Paul said, "How beautiful are the feet of those who bring glad tidings of good things" (Rom 10:15). At a day and time when feet were always dirty and nasty, he says that the carrier of the gospel has beautiful feet! It doesn't make sense unless you understand that God is not looking at feet covered with road-grime, but rather a heart that is serving Him.

David brought this point out when he wrote his classic prayer of repentance to God in Psalm 51. He acknowledged, "For Thou dost not delight in sacrifice, otherwise I would give it; Thou art not pleased with burnt offering. The sacrifices of God are a broken spirit; A broken and a contrite heart, O God, Thou wilt not despise" (vv.16-17). I can hear the Israelites whining, "But I thought sacrifices made God happy?" They meant nothing without a humble heart. What pleased God then and now is a broken and touchable heart.

What's beautiful to God is a heart that yearns to please Him with everything we do or say, no matter how little or mundane it may be. As we all know, if we make sure the little things glorify Him, the big things, whatever that may mean, will probably glorify Him also. *All means all*, and that includes home, work, school, ballfields and courts, in our cars, in the presence of others, and when it's only God and us. That's consistency, that's spiritual integrity, and that's stewardship.

55

Therefore also we have as our ambition, whether at home or absent, to be pleasing to Him. For we must all appear before the judgment seat of Christ, that each one may be recompensed for his deeds in the body, according to what he has done, whether good or bad (2 Cor 5:9-10).

USING

It's the last word in the phrase "using all our gifts," but the other words are meaningless if we don't use what God has given. Nothing that comes from God is to be rejected, ignored, buried, or regarded as meaningless. God didn't put it in these exact words, but He clearly taught the principle of "use it or lose it."

I have taught several self-defense classes through the years. I love helping people feel confident and able to break free from the chains of fear. Self-defense is survival, not being a Bruce Lee or "Walker, Texas Ranger." We all have had fantasies of kicking, twirling, and punching our way through a gang of would be attackers, but I teach the Three "R's" of self-defense, and it's not glamorous in the least. They are React, Release, and Run. The objective is to survive an assault not to beat up the bad guys.

Everyone knows how to run, and I can teach students how to release themselves from wrist grabs to headlocks, and even a full nelson. I can teach them how to incapacitate attackers who are much bigger than they are. What I can't do is prepare them for the psychological shock of being attacked. Most robbers, rapists, and attackers of any kind, depend on the victim being too shocked and surprised to respond and fight back. The paralysis that overcomes a person who is being attacked has caused folks even with a black belt in karate to become victims. It's why a large man can be overpowered by a vicious dog that's only half his size. If the person trained in self-defense is not mentally prepared to use it, he won't fare any better than the untrained victim.

What good is it if you don't use it!

God never intended for any of His gifts to us to rust out! He wants them to wear out from use!

The congregation I worked with in Texas for several years had a Christian school that met in our building at that time. Most folks thought it was wonderful that children were being taught the Word of God everyday in our building. I loved working in a building each day where I heard children singing beautiful songs about God and Jesus the way only small children can. It was also a great outreach tool, as several teens became children of God each year. But some members grumbled constantly about it. They grumbled for years, even after it was clear that it was obviously there to stay as long as they wanted to have a school there. The cry was, "They're wearing out our building!" To which I would respond, "Praise the Lord! God didn't bless us with a facility to turn it into a mausoleum or a memorial to man. Let's wear this place out in the service of God!"

When we use what God has given us — all of it — to glorify Him, it is investing in the Spirit. When Jesus said, "Do not lay up for yourselves treasures upon earth, where moth and rust destroy, and where thieves break in and steal," I don't think He was just talking about giving our money. That was certainly part of what He was talking about, but He was also talking about prayer and fasting. Actually, His subject was living for God and not for man. If we do things to receive recognition from man, that's all we will get out of it. On the other hand, if we live with integrity and walk with God even when no one is looking, God rewards those things done in secret. So invest in the Spirit! "Lay up for yourselves treasures in heaven, where neither moth nor rust destroys, and where thieves do not break in or steal; for where your treasure is, there will your heart be also" (Matt 6:19-21).

The whole point of Jesus' lesson was that it's not what
you have, but whether or not what you have is being used
to glorify God. There is nothing sinful about having only
one talent, but it is a sin to bury it (Matt 25:14-30). Everything that God has made us stewards over, which is everything He ever gave us, must be used as He intended and
thus glorify Him.

Probably the most classic passage in the New Testament
about stewardship is 1 Corinthians 4:1-2. The context of
the passage is belonging to Christ and truly being His servants. Paul said,

> Let a man regard us in this manner, as servants of Christ,
> and stewards of the mysteries of God. In this case, more-
> over, it is required of stewards that one be found trustwor-
> thy.

As powerful as the concepts of "servant" and "stewardship" are, for now, just think about the word "trustworthy." We all know that we must trust God (Prov 3:5-6), but
did you know that God trusts us? He trusts us as stewards
to properly use everything that we have in such a way that
others will realize that we are servants of God. Here's the
principle of consistency again. When things are used the
way God intended, He is glorified by that obedience. And
remember, obedience is worship to God. He trusts us to be
"a living sacrifice," total stewards, using every gift given by
Him as an act of worship that reflects positively on Him. If
we don't use it, we become untrustworthy stewards, like
the one talent man.

Are we trustworthy stewards of God's gifts? If they're
unused, we are untrustworthy. If they are not used in obedience to God, they're being abused. In the above passage,
Paul is talking about our being "stewards of the mysteries
of God." "Mysteries" are revelations or messages from God
that have not been revealed to some or all people. If we are
stewards of it, we have to know what it is. What has God

revealed to us that some people have not yet heard? That Jesus died to save them! We have been made stewards of that message and God wants us to be trustworthy. Are we?

Is the saving message of Jesus Christ something we bury the minute we step out of the church building on Sunday morning? Have we buried it from family, friends, work associates, schoolmates, and team members? If we think of worship as being one hour on Sunday, the chances are we don't think of being "stewards of the mysteries of God" as something that extends beyond the doors of the church building. Our stewardship of the message of Christ is defined as "If anyone wants it, they can come to church and get it."

Isn't it frightening to think that "use it or lose it" might be applied to the saving message of Jesus? Stewardship/ worship is using all of our gifts — for a very special purpose — to glorify God.

DISCUSSION QUESTIONS

1. If we started losing things for which we weren't thankful, what would you lose?

2. Is gratefulness essential to good stewardship? Why?

3. Is there anything that we have been given that is exempt from the responsibility of using it to glorify God?

4. What is beautiful to God?

5. Do you have any gifts from God that are "rusting" away from not being used?

CHAPTER FOUR
Stewards of Glory

I've been smitten by a curse. Not from a witch doctor or from some form of voodoo. It's from my own personal doctor, who's a friend and member of my congregation. The curse goes something like this, "Your cholesterol is a little high, so I want you to go on a high fiber, low fat diet!" Yuck! Forget the pins being stuck into dolls, I got stuck right in the stomach.

Actually, it wasn't that big of a surprise to me. I'd put on a few pounds, changed pants sizes and belt holes, and knew that I was eating too much of the bad stuff. Burgers and fries for lunch, a huge dinner followed by coffee and dessert, and a giant bowl of "Moose Tracks" ice cream before bed. (If you don't know what Moose Tracks ice cream is — please don't find out — just say "NO.") That seems like a fairly reasonable diet plan. My wife, who is a licensed and registered nutritionist, had been telling me that something would have to change sooner or later. Well,

I thought it was a multiple-choice exam, and I chose later. Wrong!

Adding fiber has not been that hard. A bowl of Raisin Bran with a little fiber supplement does the trick (though at times I'd just as soon munch on a bail of hay). The hard part is the low fat. Have you ever noticed that everything that tastes good is loaded with fat? All the juicy stuff, the sweet stuff, the fried stuff, the raw, medium, and well-done stuff, the convenience store stuff, and all the fast-food stuff — the stuff you love — IT'S LOADED WITH FAT! The stuff that makes healthy food taste good is loaded with fat. I'm one of the few people in the world who can take a healthy baked potato and drown it in so much butter that alarms go off in the State Health Department.

One of the ways I assuage my grief and Whopper™ withdrawal is to remember how much the lousy service at fast-food restaurants always irked me. I don't have to mess with that anymore. I don't have to deal with the "I hate this job and you are lucky I decided to take your order" attitude of most workers behind the counter. I don't have to deal with the smirk or look of disgust on their face when I change my order, or correct their understanding, or return my burger to have the mayo I ordered put on it. I don't have to watch them saunter over to the French fries and scoop up my order with the enthusiasm of a prisoner on trash detail.

What always bothered me the most about the poor attitudes and service was the assurance that it was not what the restaurant management wanted. Management wants happy customers because happy customers are return customers. The employees, at least some, just want a job and a pay check, and they resent having to work for minimum wages at a fast-food restaurant. Management wants smiling, people-oriented, and service-oriented workers, but the workers are thinking, "I'm not getting paid enough to smile at all these crazy people!"

That is the result of not having a clear and unified sense of purpose. The owners and management have a purpose, but they haven't been able to get the employees to buy in to it.

Unfortunately, this same problem is seen in many congregations. Many churches don't have a clear and unified sense of purpose. Why do we have churches? What is the purpose of the church? Many have gone from carrying out God's purpose to protecting the institution. Church is no longer souls but sanctuaries, services, and status quo. Is the purpose of the church simply an organized way to pull off three assemblies a week, hire a preacher, and provide a place for weddings and funerals? What are we here for?

When the major point of conflict and crisis in a church is what happens in one hour on Sunday morning, that church has lost or never had a sense of purpose. When our religion is defined by what happens or doesn't happen during that one hour, forget the purpose — we need resuscitation.

Though change is important and exhilarating, and transformation is a biblical requirement, the purpose of the church is not just change. Traditions are wonderful in terms of providing continuity and bonding within a church; maintaining traditions, however, is not the purpose of the church. The church is a body — the body of Christ, and it exists to do and be nothing less than what individual Christians are called to be. Christians are "living and holy sacrifice(s)" to God, which means that we belong to Him totally and must worship Him with our entire life. The same is true for the church. Whether separated or assembled together, everything we do and are is worship to God.

As we've already shown, worship is glorifying God, and that is something we never stop doing. *The church exists to glorify God, just as individual Christians exist to glorify God.* We do this by using all our gifts, given to us as stewards, to glorify Him.

The church doesn't exist to make the customer happy, but to save souls. The church is not an institution to be maintained, but a vehicle to glorify God. It's not our purpose to build facilities for folks to get married and buried. It's not the purpose of the church to provide security, dependability, predictability, or even excitement. Organization is a means not an end. We are neither a castle nor a clubhouse, but people who draw together, because of a common Lord, to grow, mature in Christ, and be good stewards of all God has placed in our hands.

Let's examine how we glorify God. We can't exhaust the subject in one chapter of a book because we must do everything "in the name of Jesus" and "to the glory of God" (Col 3:17, 1 Cor 10:31). We can, however, look at some of the larger essentials of what it means to glorify God. Remember, the church only glorifies God to the extent that individual Christians glorify God. So what applies to one applies to the other. We must be good stewards of our responsibility to glorify God.

WE GLORIFY GOD WHEN WE DO HIS WILL

While there may be some technical difference in terms of slant or emphasis, obedience, worship, and stewardship are synonymous terms that refer to doing the will of God. There is never a time when a child of God is not the walking, talking, and living embodiment of all three.

It doesn't take much for me to start bragging about my children. Just as you are proud of your children, I am very proud of mine. I could, no doubt, impress you with a long list of their accomplishments, awards, and commendations, but I've already told you that my greatest joy is that they love God and walk closely with Him. Still, as I reflect back through their earlier years, I was the most proud (and humbled) when they listened to my advice or followed my instructions. By listening and obeying Dad, they showed respect and love, and reflected positively on our special relationship. You could say they glorified me by their obedience to my will. And I, in turn, give all the glory to God, because I was simply trying to be the father He wanted me to be.

I think of that when I read about God's surprising pronouncement after the baptism of Jesus. Matthew records,

> . . . behold, the heavens were opened, and he saw the Spirit of God descending as a dove, *and* coming upon Him, and behold, a voice out of the heavens, saying, "This is My beloved Son, in whom I am well-pleased." (Matt 3:16-17).

This was not only a witness and confirmation from God that Jesus was His Son, but it was a pronouncement of joy over Jesus' commitment to doing His Father's will. "That's my boy, and I'm proud of him!" While it was time for His ministry as Savior to begin, Jesus had been doing His "Father's business" for a long time (Luke 2:49).

Jesus is the absolute best example of what it means to glorify God by doing His will. He made it clear that He was walking the earth for only one reason. Saving us from sin was even secondary to His major focus. Jesus was here to glorify God.

The opening sentences of Jesus' great unity prayer in John 17 explain this fully. Jesus said,

> "Father, the hour has come; glorify Thy Son, that the Son may glorify Thee, even as Thou hast given Him authority over all mankind, that to all whom Thou hast given Him, He may give eternal life. And this is eternal life, that they may know Thee, the only true God, and Jesus Christ whom Thou hast sent.
> "I glorified Thee on the earth, having accomplished the work which Thou hast given Me to do. And now, glorify Thou Me together with Thyself, Father, with the glory which I had with Thee before the world was" (John 17:1-5).

Wow! Go back and underline every place "glory," or a form of the word, is used. Glorifying God is either doing His will, or bringing His will to completion. Jesus glorified God by "accomplishing the work" God sent Him to do. Giving man the hope of eternal life was a big part of that plan, but His driving focus was doing God's will totally.

We can't do some or even most of God's will; we must do all of God's will. And just like Jesus, when we carry out His will, we glorify God. We are stewards of His will, and we are anxious to hear Him say, "Well done, good and faithful servant."

It's God's will that we get together and encourage one another with songs, prayers, study, fellowship, breaking bread, and many other things. But, it is also God's will that we be good mates, parents, workers, commuters, citizens, friends, helpers, and neighbors. He wants us to think and act like Jesus and live unselfish, compassionate lives. He wants us to witness to others that God is good, Jesus saves, and there is hope. All of this glorifies God because it's obedience, good stewardship, and it's worship.

WE GLORIFY GOD WHEN WE BEAR FRUIT

Have you ever wondered how fearful the apostles must have been as they watched Jesus cast the merchants out of the temple? The temple had its own police force, the temple guard, who must have been present when Jesus began overturning tables and chasing the moneychangers out. I can imagine the apostles standing in shock off to the side, their eyes flashing from Jesus to the temple guards, and from the temple guards to the nearest exit.

Maybe they weren't so surprised. They had just witnessed a sample of Jesus' power and authority on their walk from Bethany to Jerusalem that day. The Bible tells us that Jesus became hungry. He saw a fig tree from a distance that was green and might possibly have some fruit on it. He walked over to the tree to help Himself to a few figs, only to discover that it was fruitless. Jesus immediately cursed it by saying, "May no one ever eat fruit from you again!"

That may have been on their minds as they watched Him clean out the temple. They probably had the temple incident on their minds as they began the walk back to Bethany that evening. The gears were churning in their heads, "Who is this guy who walks in and takes control of the temple?" Just about then they passed that fig tree from that morning and noticed that it had "withered from the roots up." It wasn't just dead — it had withered! The life had been totally sucked right out of it. That got their attention (Mark 11:12-20).

God expects His creation to bear fruit. As we have already pointed out, He is praised and glorified when what He has created does what it was intended to do. Man is usually the only part of His creation that doesn't do what He intended for him to do. This lone fig tree shows us how He feels about things that don't bear fruit.

This was the thrust of Jesus' great Vine and Branches lesson in John 15. Jesus said,

> "I am the vine, you are the branches; he who abides in Me, and I in him, he bears much fruit; for apart from Me you can do nothing. If anyone does not abide in Me, he is thrown away as a branch, and dries up; and they gather them, and cast them into the fire, and they are burned. If you abide in Me, and My words abide in you, ask whatever you wish, and it shall be done for you. By this is My Father glorified, that you bear much fruit, and so prove to be My disciples" (vv. 5-8).

It's an old word, but most of us understand what it means to "abide" in Jesus. It's another word for live, dwell, or reside in. You could quote a half-dozen verses that talk about our living in Jesus or Him living in us. That's abiding!

We need to realize that to abide in Jesus means we bear fruit — period! If we don't bear fruit, we don't live in Him. And isn't it interesting that the first signs of living in Jesus and bearing fruit are study and prayer? When His words live in us, we have a healthy prayer life. Those are the two primary elements of spiritual communication: God talking to us through the Word and us talking to Him through prayer. Communication is the most important element in building any relationship, and that's true even in our relationship with God. We hear Him, He hears us, our prayers are answered, and God is glorified.

Jesus said that His Father was glorified when we "bear much fruit, and so prove to be My disciples." What kind of fruit is Jesus talking about? The context seems to define fruit bearing as keeping His commandments (v. 10). He then describes His commandment as "love one another, just as I have loved you" (v. 12). He had already pointed out that loving one another was the single most important distinguishing characteristic of His disciples (John 13:34-35). So it shouldn't be surprising to see love at the top of the list when Paul gave the fruit of the Spirit in Galatians 5:22-23.

Love has always been what God wanted from us. That makes sense, because if we love Him, we will keep His commandments. Love is not only the fruit of the Spirit, but it's the greatest gift of the Spirit (1 Cor 13). Sure, Christians bear fruit by sharing Christ with unbelievers, but isn't that a natural result of love? James said that when we "turn a sinner from the error of his way" we "save his soul from death, and will cover a multitude of sins" (5:20). Peter is the one who pointed out that "love covers a multitude of sins" (1 Pet 4:8). Weren't they talking about the same thing? So, when it comes to bearing fruit, abiding in Jesus, and glorifying God, we need to follow Paul's admonishment to "pursue love" (1 Cor 14:1).

WE GLORIFY GOD WHEN WE
CAUSE OTHERS TO GLORIFY HIM

Tom was used to being in charge of things, but at the moment, he was flat on his back in the hospital with his broken leg in traction. His neighbor, who was a member of my congregation, suggested that I visit Tom. Tom was a detective with the Washington, D.C. Metro Police Department, and since I was a police chaplain with the neighboring police department where he lived, it sort of gave us something in common.

It was a good visit. He was a very personable guy, a gung-ho cop, and really into sports. He broke his leg playing softball. So we had a lot to talk about. It turns out that he was raised a Christian, but had been inactive for a number of years due to some bad experiences with legalistic churches.

For me, it was just an enjoyable visit. For Tom, it led to some dramatic changes in his life. He came back to church, rededicated his life to Christ, and his wife became a Christian. Later, his two beautiful daughters "put on Christ" in baptism.

What can I take credit for? Nothing! God did all the work and deserves all the glory. Because of one little act of compassion, an entire family began living to glorify God.

Can you imagine a whole congregation of Christians assembling together and God not being glorified? Unthinkable! Yet it happens over and over again when brethren assemble and forget that everything they do must glorify God. One congregation that I read about had a serious struggle over assembly styles that became so nasty it caused division.

When these brethren met, they couldn't agree on which part of their assembly was more important. Each member had a favorite part and felt they had a specific gift that made their preference a higher priority than everyone else's favorite part. It was a mess. They became so selfish and self-righteous that they each did what they wanted to do during the assembly, regardless of what everyone else did. The assembly became a circus, a cacophony of noise, and a tribute to selfish pride. There was bickering and complaining, as each member thought they had the best idea for how things should happen when the church came together.

While this could easily describe many congregations today, the one I am referring to existed nearly two-thousand years ago in the town of Corinth (1 Cor 10–14). People were arguing about the assembly in the first century just like they do today, and in every case it's because they forget Who is supposed to be the center of attention. Whether it's in our personal lives or our congregational lives, God should be the focal point. It's ironic isn't it, that we unscripturally limit God to a house made by man and then act ungodly when we get there!

We are stewards of the task to do what we can to help others glorify God. That's what the assembly is all about — encouraging and edifying others! Giving to others! That is obedience and real worship. We think that our responsibility as stewards in the assembly begins and ends with a check in the collection plate. Stewardship is a life of worship to God that began at conversion and ends when our body returns to dust. We don't stop being stewards when we enter into a gathering of brethren. Our traditional mindset of being judgmental, critical, do-for-me spectators at the assembly is one of Satan's greatest victories.

Paul told the Corinthian brethren, "do not be children in your thinking; yet in evil be babes, but in your thinking be mature" (1 Cor 14:20). Spiritually mature people think of others and their needs. They are loving, considerate, thoughtful, and unselfish. They don't insist on their own way. They want everyone else's buttons pushed rather than their own. Paul told them that when an unbelieving visitor sees that kind of Christlike spirit among brethren, "he will fall on his face and worship God, declaring that God is certainly among you" (v. 25).

God is worshiped and glorified when we are obedient to Him. When we are obedient to Him, we are being good stewards. When we help or cause others to glorify God, it's worship, obedience, and stewardship in action.

This leads us to another question. Are we glorifying God if our real motivation for doing something is to receive attention and praise for ourselves? Jesus said, "Beware of practicing your righteousness before men to be noticed by them; otherwise you have no reward with your Father who is in heaven" (Matt 6:1). He went on to point out that if we pray, fast, and give to receive man's praises, that is the only reward we will get.

Our obedience to God should point others in His direction. Every word we speak and every action we take reflects on our Father. We live to glorify Him, and that means others should notice it. How can we be "the salt of the earth" and "the light of the world" if no one ever notices that we live for God? That is why Jesus declared, "Let your light shine before men in such a way that they may see your good works, and glorify your Father who is in heaven" (Matt 5:13-16).

People need to see that Jesus has made a difference in our lives. We don't want them to be impressed with us. That's self-righteousness! We want them to see the power behind the difference, and glorify God.

WE GLORIFY GOD WHEN WE ARE UNITED

God is love (1 John 4:8). The single most important distinguishing characteristic that shows we are disciples of Jesus is that we love one another (John 13:35). Loving one another is how we love God (1 John 4:7). So what does it say about us and our relationship with God when we don't

71

show love for one another? It doesn't say anything good, that's for sure!

There isn't much disunity about doctrine anymore, at least within the church. I can't remember the last time I heard a heated discussion of "one Lord, one faith, one baptism, one God and Father of all who is over all and through all and in all" (Eph 4:5-6). On the other hand, most of the controversies in the church during the last ten years have been over preferences. The people who have broken their unity with their local congregation didn't do it because of the lack of baptisms or benevolence, but because their personal preference buttons were not being pushed during one hour on Sunday morning.

Some became hateful and belligerent, and with righteous indignation, stormed away from their church family in search of the right group of button pushers. Loving the brethren took back seat to predictability or some new feelgood innovation. Churches that attempt to be tolerant and moderate in their changes, lose folks at both ends of the extreme preference scale.

I worked with a church in Texas that tried to be a middle-of-the-road church, in terms of trying to keep everybody happy, and we managed to double the size of the local conservative church and the progressive church. People were determined to get what they wanted or they'd take their ball and go play elsewhere.

We are stewards who have the responsibility to glorify God with everything He has given us. He saved us, adopted us, and placed us in His church with all His people. One of our primary tasks as stewards is to be "diligent to preserve the unity of the Spirit in the bond of peace" (Eph 4:3). God is glorified when that happens. Unfortunately, we are far more diligent about getting our way than we are about making sure He gets His way.

Don't get confused. These last four chapters have been hammering home the point that worship, obedience, and stewardship involve our total lives. But unity, by its very nature, is a togetherness problem. If we were never together, which some have adopted as a lifestyle, unity wouldn't be any challenge at all. Because we are together, out of obedience to God's command to encourage, equip, and edify one another, unity is a problem. Among the attitudes that make unity a problem are the following:

+ we forget that our purpose is to glorify God;
+ we ignore our responsibility to be good stewards of God's gifts;
+ we relegate brotherly love to an option;
+ we have a tradition of please-me-first in our assemblies;
+ we made the assembly The Worship and loaded it down with formalism, traditions, reverential atmosphere, and made it the focal point of our religion;
+ we want relevance more than we want tolerance;
+ we want to feel good more than we want to help others feel good;
+ we stopped celebrating grace and started maintaining the status quo;
+ the assembly is an obligation rather than an opportunity;
+ we decided that fellowship was an extracurricular church activity that is secondary and inferior to the "Formal Worship";
+ the number of personal preferences is as large as the number in attendance;
+ we want to get our ticket punched and get to Luby's™ before the Methodists;
+ church is the only place in your world that hasn't changed, and you savor that dependability and predictability;
+ you want change and no one else seems to want it;
+ you want things to stay the same and everyone else seems determined to change things;

✦ that one hour on Sunday morning provides you with the sum total of all your spiritual study, prayer, giving, praising God, and paying Him back for all He's done for you;

✦ you think the traditions you love so dearly are based on Scripture;

✦ you think the changes you long for are based on Scripture;

✦ we are unwilling to be Christlike.

I love traditions and I love change, but I love Jesus more than either one of those preferences. There are two primary reasons why I have written so much about worship (this is the third book). First, we must have a true and accurate understanding of what the New Testament teaches on this subject. It has been a sacred cow too long and our traditions have turned a simple get-together into a legalistic and ritualistic act of faith, filled with man-made ordinances, rituals, and requirements.

But secondly, when we understand that our whole life is worship to God; that we are stewards of every gift, every breath, and every blessing; and that we exist to glorify Him, which means that we have been feasting on His Word and communicating with Him all day every day; then each one of us will conclude, *"I don't have to have what I want that one hour on Sunday morning!"*

When do we practice the "one another" passages if it's not when we are together? If we don't practice them when we are together, then they are merely theory or powerless theology to us. When do you love, forgive, bear burdens, be devoted, give preference, and greet with a kiss if it's not in the assembly? When do the strong accept and give in to the weak if it's not when we are together? When do you determine "not to put an obstacle or a stumbling block in a brother's way" if you are never with them? (Rom 14:13).

We need to remember who we live for and belong to. As Paul stated, "For not one of us lives for himself, and not one dies for himself; for if we live, we live for the Lord, or

74

if we die, we die for the Lord; therefore whether we live or die, we are the Lord's" (Rom 14:7-8).

If we live or die for the Lord, can't we be tolerant and unselfish for the Lord? Can we sing songs others like, change the order of the assembly, and try something different (or the same) for the sake of the brethren? The grateful and humble servant of God looks for opportunities to say, "I want to do whatever helps you walk closer to God." That's much better than name-calling or self-righteous judgments that alienate others and place our own souls in jeopardy. Remember Paul's warning in Romans 14:10,

> But you, why do you judge your brother? Or you again, why do you regard your brother with contempt? For we shall all stand before the judgment seat of God.

Let me throw out one more concept about unity. To some it is a dirty word and to others it's politics and not religion at all. I'm talking about compromise — not compromising Scripture or any spiritual truth, but the willingness to meet someone halfway, as opposed to being closed minded. Tolerance is the willingness to accept others and their differences. For a Christian, it may mean totally giving in to another's wishes and needs. Compromise is a form of tolerance. In any and all areas of preference, areas where God has given us the freedom to do whatever works best or is expedient, Christians should be willing to compromise.

Because of mistrust and our heritage of paranoia, most Christians don't want to compromise. "Once you open the door," some say, "who knows how many other wild cats will slip in!" The classic church phobia is "Who knows what this will lead to?" It could lead to something wonderful if we trust in Jesus instead of our ability to define and defend preferential orthodoxy.

I have witnessed and even been the instigator of some wonderful compromises between brethren in terms of blending assembly preferences. Many times it doesn't have to be an either/or proposition, but a both/and proposition. For example, we had a huge clash between those who wanted to sing hymns during the passing of the communion trays and those who wanted only quiet meditation time. Does the New Testament tell us what we can and can't do during the passing of the communion elements? Not a word. It only tells us what to reflect on, not how or how long to do it (1 Cor 11:23-29). Most folks read their Bibles, read/sing a hymn, or pray. The same passage that gives permission to do that gives permission to sing "On a hill far away, stood an old rugged cross." (Someone actually told me that that distracted them during communion. "The Old Rugged Cross" took their mind off of the Cross? Go figure!)

The shepherds decided that we would have quiet meditation during the first half of the passing of the trays. When they got halfway to the back, we started a song. It was a simple compromise that worked well (except for the few people on both sides who felt like they lost their battle).

As stewards of unity, each one of us must be diligent and unselfish. If we get our way but God isn't glorified, what have we really gained? Serving others as stewards of God means submitting to others. We need to love each other more than we love our preferences. Peter said it best as he pulled it all together in 1 Peter 4:8-11,

> Above all, keep fervent in your love for one another, because love covers a multitude of sins. Be hospitable to one another without complaint. As each one has received a *special* gift, employ it in serving one another, as good stewards of the manifold grace of God. Whoever speaks, let *him speak,* as it were, the utterances of God; whoever serves, *let him do so* as by the strength which God supplies; so that in all things God may be glorified through Jesus Christ, to whom belongs the glory and dominion forever and ever. Amen.

PULLING-IT-ALL-TOGETHER THOUGHTS

The Golden Arches of McDonald's™ have been around nearly as long as I have. When they opened their restaurant in Washington, D.C. I was a youngster, and I couldn't get enough of their French fries. Unfortunately, I still can't. Throughout the years they have had some of the most entertaining commercials on TV. A good friend of mine was in one of their first breakfast commercials, but it wasn't my favorite one. My favorite McDonald's commercials all had the memorable jingle, "You deserve a break today. So get out and get away — to McDonald's." I sang it all the time. Even now, many years later, I will find myself humming the tune or singing the song in the shower.

"You deserve a break today?" I wonder — when do you ever get a break from being a Christian? Do we deserve a break from church? Is there such a thing as a vacation from godliness?

Silly questions — right? Everyone knows that being a Christian is total involvement. Church is us — each one of us — wherever we are and whomever we are with. Godliness is a character issue not a worship hour. It's either in our hearts and what we are, or it's not.

The point of these last four chapters has been to emphasize the totality of spirituality. It's all or nothing. We are worshiping beings. Beings that are living sacrifices to God. The sacrifice never ends and neither does worship. It's what we are. This worship is best defined by the concept of stewardship because stewardship is the commitment to glorifying God with everything He's given us. Worship/stewardship is using all our gifts to glorify God whether they're tiny and insignificant or something seen by the whole world. Worship is total stewardship, which is totally glorifying God.

We do everything "to the glory of God" and "in the name of Jesus." There is no break from such an awesome responsibility. After all, God doesn't take any breaks from watching over us!

DISCUSSION QUESTIONS

1. In what ways do we send out mixed signals to the world about the purpose of the church?

2. God is glorified when we do His will, but how do we determine what His will is?

3. What are some of the ways that we "bear fruit" for God?

4. Is it possible to love and serve God separately and apart from loving and serving others? How?

5. When do we get a break from glorifying God?

CHAPTER FIVE
Stewards of Trust

There are not many of us around. At least I haven't met very many. I'm talking about people who were born and raised in our nation's capital, Washington, D.C. I always had a sense of being in a very powerful city — a city that, to a certain degree, was the center of the world. It also gave me a great sense of history. I grew up seeing the Capitol, the White House, the Lincoln and Jefferson Memorials, and spent many days wandering through the many museums that surrounded the Mall. We used to race to the top of the Washington Monument and wade in the reflection pool. One of my most favorite places to walk through was Arlington National Cemetery. I still watch in awe at the changing of the guard before the Tomb of the Unknown Soldier.

As a youngster, my family used to attend a church in the middle of downtown Washington — on the corner of 10th and G Street to be exact. When I went by myself on the bus, I got off the bus in front of the old FBI Building and I had to walk past Ford's Theater and the Peterson House to get to the church building. I also had to walk past a huge cathedral with ornate designs and giant spires.

One day, as I strolled past the cathedral, I could tell something unusual was going on there. Hundreds of people crowded the yard in front of the building, clearly waiting expectantly for someone to come out of the building. I had to stop and see what it was all about. In just a minute or two, the front doors of the cathedral opened wide and a Catholic priest stepped out dressed in a flowing reddish-purple robe with a large bullet shaped hat on his head. He also carried a tall pole with a cross on the top of it. I knew at once that this was a visiting Cardinal of the Catholic Church.

I was in awe of the whole scene, but especially the priest in his priestly garb. He looked so official, so powerful, and even so spiritual. Everyone was bowing and struggling to just touch him. I'd never seen anything like that, and I was impressed. I thought, "It must be nice to be a priest."

Many years later I discovered an exciting New Testament principle that today is still one of the most overlooked roles and blessings for every Child of God. We are all priests! Not just any priest, but "a royal priesthood, a holy nation, a people for *God's* own possession, that you may proclaim the excellencies of Him who has called you out of darkness into His marvelous light" (1 Pet 2:9).

A priest was set apart for holy duty for God. They offered sacrifices for individuals and the nation. They had access to God. They represented God. All of these things are now descriptions of what every Christian is and does. We are "a living and holy sacrifice, acceptable to God," (Rom 12:1) and we confidently know that "if we ask anything according to His will, He hears us" (1 John 5:14). We have direct access to God anywhere, any time, and for any reason. And we represent Him as His children, His ambassadors, and the image of His Son, who lives in us (Phil 1:21).

A priest had only one purpose and that was to serve God. Everybody understood that. Now everybody who is in a covenant relationship with God is a priest. A priest never stopped being a priest. He was born into it and died a priest. He was a steward of God's will. He lived to glorify God through obedience to Him. What a privilege. As the little country boy said, "Now I are one!"

TOWERS OF TRUSTWORTHINESS

Priests were entrusted by God with carrying out His will. They were not only expected to follow all the rules and regulations of the Law, but to internalize the spirit of God's will. God was just as displeased with Old Covenent priests who turned His will into meaningless, mindless ritualism as He is with New Covenant priests who turn grace into a one-day-a-week pilgrimage. God has always wanted His priests to be consistently holy and obedient. It's always been a heart thing!

God has always placed a lot of trust in the hands of His servants — His priests. As His priests we are His hands, feet, eyes, and mouth. He trusts us to do His will, share His will, and live His will. So we are students of His will, as we've already studied, but we are also stewards of His trust. As the passage we've already looked at states, "it is required of stewards that one be found trustworthy" (1 Cor 4:2).

It is up to us, as stewards of God's will, not only to be obedient, but to let His will become our will. We want His spirit in our hearts and not just to go through the motions of doing what we are supposed to do. Holiness is a goal of the heart as well as a standard to live by. The challenge is to fold Him into our hearts, our conscience, and our very souls. We have a relationship, but we also have His indwelling. After

81

all, isn't that what God has always wanted? From the beginning He has wanted us to "love the Lord your God with all your heart and with all your soul and with all your might" (Deut 6:5).

No one can do that for us or force it to happen. It's a matter of choice, and He trusts us to make the right choice, to accept His will. If others don't understand it or are too legalistic to accept it — so be it. We can't violate the trust He has placed in us.

When we think of Old Testament priests, we often think of untrustworthy men like Nadab and Abihu, who were struck dead for offering strange fire before the Lord (Num 3:4). Or perhaps we think of Aaron allowing the Israelites to construct and worship the golden calf (Exod 32). Or maybe you remember the Hebrew prophets who hammered the priests for being greedy, uncaring, "yes men" for the king.

There's an incident in the life of David where the priests were the real heroes of the day. They were trustworthy stewards of God's will even though they were lied to and deceived by David.

Saul had tried to kill David several times and in several ways and failed every time. His pursuit of David was in earnest, and David was running for his life. In 1 Samuel 21, David came to the town of Nob and asked Ahimelech the priest for help. He told them that he was on a secret mission for the king when in reality he was running from the king.

The priests all knew (I believe) that David had been anointed to be the next king, so in their minds helping David was the will of God, and they were deeply concerned with making sure it was followed. They were more than willing to help. They began by giving David the only bread they had, which was the consecrated bread, which was also called the Shewbread or the Bread of the Presence. This was holy bread kept in a holy place and wasn't to be eaten by anyone but the priests. But God's will for that moment made giving it to David a higher priority. Jesus would later use that as an example of human needs and compassion being a higher priority than ceremonial laws (Matt 12, Mark 2, Luke 6).

Next they gave him the sword of Goliath; he had probably given it to them after his victory over the giant so it could be dedicated to God. Now there was a change of plans. He needed a weapon, so they gave it back to him. As he lifted the heavy sword in his hands, it must have brought back memories of that famous day when he delivered Israel from its enemies. It also reminded him that if God was on his side, he couldn't lose.

It's debatable whether Ahimelech and the other priests knew they were placing themselves at risk by aiding a fugitive whom the king was trying to catch and destroy. It's hard to believe that they knew nothing about the efforts Saul had made in the past to destroy David, but either way, they would have followed God's will at all cost.

When Saul heard about their actions, he summoned them to come before him. When he challenged them, Ahimelech, who mentioned nothing about David's misrepresentation of the truth, defended David's loyalty and pointed out that he had been praying for David for a long time. Saul, incensed by their loyalty to God rather than him, had Ahimelech and the other priests killed — eighty-five of God's priests. He also had the rest of the residents of Nob and their livestock put to death (1 Samuel 22).

God's priests paid the ultimate sacrifice for being trustworthy to God. They helped to save the Lord's anointed and lost their lives in the process. They were total stewards — trustworthy stewards, even if David wasn't as honest as he should have been.

A trustworthy steward is generous, and in the Lord's service that means first giving yourself. The priests of Nob were like the Christians in Macedonia who were described by Paul as being generous because they first gave themselves (2 Cor 8:1-5). Once you give yourself to God, being a total steward is not so difficult. Their attitude was that everything they had was God's, so giving it to God's anointed was no problem for them.

I especially like the fact that they understood what it was they were entrusted with. They were entrusted with doing God's will, not maintaining the status quo. When God's will involved changing their plans, they changed. They didn't scream "We've never done that before," or "What will this lead to?" When God calls for change, his stewards change; they don't cry "foul" or live by fear, or settle for failure. When God wanted untouchable bread to be touched, they touched it. When He wanted a dedicated sword to be given away, they gave it away. When they were called on to die for the Lord's Anointed, they died.

How could they do all that? Trust! God trusted them and they trusted Him. They knew, as Abraham did about Isaac, that God could raise them from the dead if He willed it.

Real worship is being a steward of trust.

THE TROUBLE WITH TRUST

Trust is a precious gift. There is no relationship that doesn't require it. There have probably been more marriages broken, children alienated, and friendships destroyed because of violated trust than any other cause. Trust makes up for what we don't see and can't know. We trust others because we can't know for sure what is on their minds, and what they are doing when we're not around. When that trust is betrayed, it is extremely painful and destructive.

We live by trust because the only other alternative is fear. We trust that all oncoming traffic will stay on their side of the road. We trust our water to be clean, our bank teller to be accurate, and our counselor to keep confidences. We trust that our government won't ignore our rights, our doctor knows what he is talking about, and our church leaders care about our souls.

We crave trust. We want to be trusted by our spouse, our children, our employer, our church, our government, and our friends. We want the security and joy of knowing we can trust them. Trust is essential. That's why lying, cheating, gossip, dishonesty, and infidelity hurt so much. Trust is broken — violated — cheapened — defiled.

We can understand that so easily when others violate our trust in them. Somehow we don't see it as easily when it comes to our breaking a trust ourselves. For some reason, it's even harder for us to understand how God feels when we break the trust He has placed in us.

For example, have you ever found yourself thinking, "I don't understand the Israelites? If I had witnessed the ten plagues that God sent on Egypt, had my firstborn saved by lamb's blood, seen God stop Pharaoh's army with a pillar of fire, walked on the dry sea floor after Moses parted the water, and watched as God destroyed the pursuing soldiers, I'd never have built and worshiped a golden calf! That's incredible! How could they do that after all God had done for them? How could they forget so quickly all of God's blessings?"

The golden calf was an idol to the forgotten God! Yet, how quickly we forget! God blessed us with a plan for our redemption even before He created our world. He blessed us with life and gave us every breath we've taken since then. We have more material blessings than any people who have ever lived, and we turn that blessing into a golden calf of our own making. God is forgotten as we worship materialism, careers, pleasure, comfort, and convenience.

He is forgotten even when we meet together in His name as we push, politic, and pout to get what we want in "our worship services." He is forgotten when our preferences are elevated above His will and when brotherly love is secondary to change or keeping the status quo.

Is it possible that God has blessed us too much? Are blessings a hindrance or obstacles to walking with God rather than a tool for bonding more closely with Him? Can we be trusted to be good stewards of so much? Increased blessings mean increased responsibility. Have we been given more than we are capable of handling obediently?

What's the problem with blessings? We need to examine this briefly so that we will know what is getting in the way of our worship to God as good stewards of His gifts.

COMPLACENCY

One of the biggest problems with a lifetime of great blessings is that we come to expect them. We assume that since we've always had them, they will always be available and continuous. We have taken God's blessings for granted for so long that we've become complacent about what He does for us.

Complacency is just another word for ingratitude. Because we have a lifestyle of ingratitude, we don't dwell on how blessed we are or how undeserving we are. I am convinced that this is why so many people who declare themselves Christians are so unprepared for life's disasters. When some tragedy comes into their lives, they are devastated and blame God. They can only see what they have lost rather than what they have had.

If you are thankful for every day that God has given you and you treasure every blessing that allows you to enjoy life and loved ones, you don't fall apart when the inevitable happens. How many years of good health has God given you? How much of it did you deserve, earn, or feel worthy of? Not one single day! You knew from the moment you discovered your mortality that good health could not last forever. So why are you shocked and embittered when you find out that your body is falling apart? Why get angry over what you will lose or not be able to do? If you've been thankful to God through the years, you'll be thankful that it didn't happen many years ago. You will be thankful for what God blessed you with instead of blaming Him for cheating you out of something you never deserved.

There is nothing more painful than the death of a loved one. Most of us joke about hoping that we die before our spouse does, but we're not joking. We'd rather face our own death than deal with the hurt and separation from one we love so much. But you know what? It's going to happen. It's not a question of whether but when. So how much time do you deserve to be together? Do you deserve to go first or second? Do you deserve to go before your children do? How many years do they deserve to live?

Jesus is still the only answer. Because we walk with Him and prepare for eternity with Him, all else is gravy. We need to start right now being thankful for what God has given us. Don't blame Him if you haven't spent the time building relationships, enjoying togetherness, and creating eternal memories. "Someday" is the ultimate sign of complacency. Even Jesus told us to live for today "for tomorrow will care for itself. Each day has enough trouble of its own" (Matt 6:34).

Complacency is pride. It's being focused on self and not God. When we don't think in terms of what God has given us but rather what we have, own, and possess, we've become proud. What does it mean that "God opposes the proud?" I am not sure, and I don't want to find out. What might happen to the individual whom God is opposed to? What might God do to drive pride out of our hearts? What ever it might be, the end result that God is looking for is humility. A complacent person is not a humble person.

That was the message Jesus wanted us to glean from the story of the "certain rich man" whose land was "very productive." You remember the story. He looked at his amazing windfall and started talking about what "I shall do." He planned to expand his storage units and build some newer and bigger ones. He was so pleased with his good fortune and his plans that he said, "And I will say to my soul, 'Soul, you have many goods laid up for many years *to come*; take your ease, eat, drink *and* be merry.'" But God had other ideas. He told the ungrateful farmer that his life would end that very night. And He asked him, "*Now* who will own what you have prepared?" Just in case we think this is a story for the proverbial "other guy," God added, "So is the man who lays up treasure for himself, and is not rich toward God" (Luke 12:16-21).

If our response to blessings is complacency, we need to remember that complacency equals pride, pride brings God's opposition, and God's opposition brings — who knows what! For this man it was death.

FORGETFULNESS

Moses was a hundred and twenty years old. He'd been the leader of God's people for forty years and now it was time for him to turn the reins of leadership over to Joshua. It was also time for him to go and be with God. He turned the Law over to the sons of Levi, the priests, and he commissioned Joshua for his new task. He had them call all the people together for one last message from Moses before he left to see the Promised Land from the mountaintop.

He was not happy with the people. He called them rebellious and stubborn and warned that they would become worse after his death. He sang them a song of praise to God, of remembrance, and of warning. One of the indictments and warnings was,

You neglected the Rock who begot you,
And forgot the God who gave you birth (Deut. 32:18).

Forgetting what God has done is not new to us. His people have struggled with short memories ever since Adam and Eve thought they could hide from God. While forgetfulness is very closely related to complacency, forgetfulness has some characteristics that set it apart as a serious problem. Complacency, as mentioned, is a problem with pride, while forgetfulness is a lack of focus, intensity, and personal reflection. Like complacency, it is selfishness, but it's more from thoughtlessness than arrogant assumptions.

Isn't it amazing that when things go wrong we quickly scream, "Why, God?" But when things go well, which they do most of the time, we forget to say, "Thank you, Lord?" It is easy to think of forgetfulness as merely accidental memory loss, but it is often just a form of the sin of ingratitude.

Have you ever thanked God for all the wonderful memories you have? Don't you have a wealth of beautiful memories from your childhood? Christmas with your family, Thanksgiving dinners, trips together, playing games, school, sports, Bible classes, VBS, summer camps, childhood friends, church fellowships, songs, clothes, and thousands of other experiences. Were they not gifts from God? Why have you forgotten all those things and who gave them to you? Why is it that today's problems overshadow yesterday's blessings? How can one painful experience cause us to forget a lifetime of blessings?

We haven't been developing a grateful spirit all along the way as we should have been. The great part is that it's never too late to be grateful if we choose to be grateful.

Once, when Jesus was traveling between Samaria and Galilee on His way to Jerusalem, He suddenly heard several men calling out His name. Ten men had come out to meet Him, but they had to do it from a distance. They were all lepers – the most alienated people of society at that time. They were unclean, unwanted, and untouchable. When they heard that Jesus was coming their way, they rushed out to see if He could do anything to release them from their life sentence of pain, misery, and loneliness.

They had to shout because of the distance they were forced to keep and to make sure their voices were heard beyond the hand they held in front of their face to signify that they were unclean. They yelled, "Jesus, Master, have mercy on us!" As He looked at the pitiful group of outcasts, He immediately decided to help them.

Jesus told them to "Go and show yourselves to the priests." There must have been something in the way He said it, a smile or a twinkle in His eye, because they suddenly had a sense of hope. At some point in the trip to the temple to see the priest, they realized that they were cleansed. The leprosy was gone and their skin was as new as a baby's. The shouts of joy echoed through the hills and valleys as ten men were given a new chance at life.

One of them, as soon as he realized that he'd been healed, did an about-face and returned to thank Jesus. He glorified God with loud praises and fell on his face at the feet of Jesus, thanking Him profusely. Jesus' only question was "Were there not ten cleansed? But the nine — where are they? Was no one found who turned back to give glory to God, except this foreigner?"

That's a reasonable thing to ask. What happened to the other nine? How could they possibly forget to give thanks and glorify God for His wonderful blessing of healing? Part of the answer is found in Jesus' admonition to the one returning former leper. He told him, "Rise, and go your way; your faith has made you well" (Luke 17:11-19).

Was Jesus talking about the man's faith in "going" to the priest as being the faith that made him well? That means that they all had faith and all ten were healed because of that faith. Maybe He wasn't even talking about the healing from leprosy. Maybe He was referring to some other malady when He said that his faith made him well. Was He talking about spiritual wellness? Was this lone grateful foreigner declared spiritually well by Jesus because He didn't forget to thank the One who healed him? I've never heard that interpretation of this story before, but it seems like an appropriate one to me. Especially when it comes between Jesus' talking about our being "unworthy slaves" (v. 10) and the dangers of ignoring "the kingdom of God . . . in your midst" (v. 21).

We all know that God wants us to glorify Him by being good stewards of every gift He has given us. As we've been saying, that's what real worship is. But, what if we forget to be good stewards? What if we forget to thank Him for all His wonderful gifts? How does it make Him feel?

Peter encouraged us to grow spiritually in response to the goodness of God. He said, "His divine power has granted to us everything pertaining to life and godliness, through the true knowledge of Him who called us by His own glory and excellence." Because He has given us every-thing we need, we should strive to thrive in diligence, faith, courage, knowledge, self-control, perseverance, godliness, brotherly kindness, and love. These are the things that will cause us to grow and be fruitful for the Lord. Why wouldn't we want to grow in all these "Christian Graces"?

Peter answers that question. "For he who lacks these *qualities* is blind *or* short-sighted, having forgotten *his* purification from his former sins" (2 Pet 1:3-9). Lack of spiri-tual growth is a sure sign of forgetfulness. When we became children of God, the blood of Jesus Christ His Son cleansed us from all our sins. They were washed away and totally for-gotten by God. Something that only He is able to do — holy forgetfulness. Our former sins simply don't exist anymore! Incredible! Amazing! Unforgettable? Unfortunately, we sometimes forget what God has done for us. We honor His holy forgetfulness with our unholy forgetfulness!

GREED AND COVETOUSNESS

Remember the old TV commercial selling potato chips, the one that issued the challenge, "Bet you can't eat just one"? It's not only an excellent illustration for lack of control, but it's a good illustration of greed. One of the problems with blessings is the selfish tendency to always want more. Rather than feel grateful for what we have been given, we yearn for bigger and better things. Not only do we want more, but we want what others have. Our selfishness and greed lead us to believe that everyone else has better blessings than we do. So we feel cheated, and believe that the world, and God, owe us. Satan has an amazing ability to make people respond to God's continued blessings with greed instead of gratitude.

In Tolstoy's book *Man and Dame*, the hero is told that he will be given all the land that he can plow a single furrow around in one day. He is excited and starts off with great energy and enthusiasm. He determined to only circle an amount of land that he knew he could easily cover in the allotted time. But as the day progressed, he began to want more of what he was looking at, so he made a bigger circle. He plowed and plowed and began to wander off track to the point that he couldn't find his original point of departure. He panicked and struggled even harder and faster until he dropped dead with a heart attack. The only land he secured was a four-by-six plot in which to be buried.[9]

Jesus said, "Beware, and be on your guard against every form of greed; for not *even* when one has an abundance does his life consist of his possessions" (Luke 12:15). The drive to accumulate possessions, to want what others have, and to be judged by our junk is ingratitude gone to seed. Satan loves it because it's impossible to be living worship for God when you're living to worship the next new shiny thing to come along. Which brings us to our final problem with blessings.

IDOLATRY

He was sharp, good looking, and rich. He also thought of himself as righteous, but it was only a façade. With a bounce in his step he walked up to Jesus and boldly asked, "Good Teacher, what shall I do to obtain eternal life?" You probably recognize him as the man we call the Rich Young Ruler in Luke 18:18-25. He beamed when told to keep the Ten Commandments because he'd been doing that since childhood. When Jesus told him to sell all his possessions, give the money to the poor, and come follow Him, it didn't sit too well. In fact, it made him sad because he knew immediately that he loved his things more than His King.

That's idolatry. It's not just bowing down to a golden calf or kissing the foot of a marble statue of Zeus. It's valuing anything as worth more to us than God. Another way to define idolatry is that it's allowing anything to come between us and God. When this world's goods become more valuable to us than this world's God, we are idolatrous people.

How would you feel if your child's love for you was transferred to something you gave her? Suppose you gave your teenager a car and he made it clear that it was more important to him than you were? You say, "That's crazy! How could they love the gift more than the giver?" You wouldn't like it. In fact, it would be very painful for you to see such a change of love take place. It would be a serious problem for your relationship.

We do that to God, don't we? He gives and gives, and we love the gifts so much that we seek more instead of recognizing His goodness and generosity. That's what the Gentiles had done with God's blessings. They looked at all He had done and ignored Him. Paul warned us:

> For even though they knew God, they did not honor Him
> as God, or give thanks; but they became futile in their spec-
> ulations, and their foolish heart was darkened. Professing

93

to be wise, they became fools, and exchanged the glory of the incorruptible God for an image in the form of corruptible man and of birds and four-footed animals and crawling creatures. Therefore God gave them over in the lusts of their hearts to impurity, that their bodies might be dishonored among them. For they exchanged the truth of God for a lie, and worshiped and served the creature rather than the Creator, who is blessed forever (Rom. 1:21-25).

Any time we value something created by the Creator more than the Creator Himself, it's idolatry. It's worshiping the blessing more than the Blesser. He gives us health, and we worship our bodies; He gives us careers, and we live for our jobs; He gives us luxuries, and we devote ourselves to obtaining more. The blessings become blemishes, and the gifts become gods.

THE BLESSING OF BLESSINGS

Remember the Cowardly Lion in "The Wizard of Oz" singing his famous solo, "If I Were the King of the Forrrrrrest"? The basic theme of the song was that if he were king things would all go his way. We all find ourselves wishing we were king of our forest because we'd all like to have things go our way. Just think about it for a second. If we can't learn to be thankful and humble with what we have now, what makes us think we'd be better at it as a king? Humility is not usually something that you think of when you think of kings.

David was an exception. Not a perfect exception, but still an exception. I love to visualize the most powerful man in the Middle East, walking along the walls of Jerusalem viewing his city and his people and stopping to look up into the night sky. The vastness of the universe overwhelms him. Instead of being full of himself, he is full of gratitude and humility. As he looks above he says,

94

When I consider Thy heavens, the work of Thy fingers,
The moon and the stars, which Thou hast ordained;
What is man, that Thou dost take thought of him?
And the son of man, that Thou dost care for him?
O Lord, our Lord,
How majestic is Thy name in all the earth! (Psalm 8:3-4,9).

He had it all, yet he was humbled by God's majesty and power. He knew that it was all given to man so that man would glorify God. He realized that man didn't deserve any of it, yet God "made him a little lower than God, And dost crown him with glory and majesty!" (v. 5). How could man be anything but grateful and humble?

Remember the secret to being an obedient steward of God's gifts. It begins with gratitude, which creates a sense of indebtedness to God. When we then realize we can never repay God for all He has done, we are humbled. Humility empowers us to be unselfish and sacrificial and be truly Christlike. Since "God gives grace to the humble," our gratitude increases and it all starts again. And that is real living worship to God.

DISCUSSION QUESTIONS

1. What does it mean to you to know that Christians are priests? (1 Pet 2:9)

2. On your list of essential elements in a relationship, how high would trust be on the list? Why?

3. How important is trust when it comes to being a good steward?

4. In what ways do we violate God's trust?

5. How, when, and why could blessings be a problem?

CHAPTER SIX
Stewards of Our Minds

Everyone has heard the old joke about the hen and the hog who discuss making a ham-and-eggs breakfast for their farmer. The hog points out that the hen is making a contribution, but for him it's total commitment. It's worn but worthy. The last five chapters have been dealing with the total commitment God expects from us. Worship is total. We are living sacrifices, which means total obedience. Because God is glorified by our obedient worship to Him, we therefore live to glorify Him. Stewardship embodies all of these concepts — especially when we understand that we are stewards of everything God has given to us. We are like the hog and not the hen. Ours is total commitment, not a contribution.

Jesus was the ultimate steward of God's will. As we've seen, He "emptied Himself" and became a living and literal sacrifice to God. He needs to be our mental picture of what stewardship is all about. If you are like me, when I hear the word "steward" I automatically think of waiters in white jackets hustling to fulfill your every whim, and hopefully earn a generous tip. If you've never experienced being waited on hand and foot, you need to take one of the many ocean cruises sometime. They really know how to make you feel special with your own waiter, busboy, cabin steward, and an army of others just waiting to be beckoned. You paid for it, and you'll pay even more at the end of the cruise as you hand out several tip-filled envelopes.

Christian stewardship certainly involves being a servant — even a waiter at times, but it's a way of life not a vocation. You can't go to it and then leave it. It's not a matter of a certain number of hours on a certain day of the week. It's what we are. We live to glorify God through consistent obedience to His will. As we just studied, we are stewards of His will. We are stewards of everything — every minute of every day.

Stewardship is not just doing a good job or being productive. It includes that because we want to do our best for God. Solomon told us, "Whatever your hand finds to do, verily, do *it* with all your might" (Eccl 9:10). But we are not God's employees; we are His children. He isn't uninterested in our performance and productivity, but He wants it to come from a heart that loves Him completely — heart, soul, mind, and strength. Like a loving parent, He wants to see our crayon drawing from school, but He wants to know if we learned something, if we're growing, and if we are closer to being like Jesus.

God wants to see us carry our cross, like Jesus, but He wants us to be like Jesus in that we empty ourselves first. A godly steward wants his whole life to be worship to God. Godly stewardship isn't just giving, it's being a giver — a sharing, cheerful, submissive, and sacrificial giver. We want to hear Him say "Good job," but we also want to hear him say, "Good life!"

God's steward says in his or her heart, "Father, I want

what you want! I'm ready for anything that you need me to do or be." It needs to be an honest declaration. If you want to give your church leaders a heart attack, just tell them about your godly "declaration of dependence." We sing "Thou art the potter; I am the clay," but the truth is we don't want God doing any molding on us. Many just want to be left alone. They don't volunteer, and they don't want to be asked. Even those who accept responsibilities in service to God and His church resent it. They think, "Why me? Give me a break! Can we find a replacement?" They are not stewards; they are on a religious cruise ship and want to be served rather than to do the serving.

Godly stewards look at their responsibilities and say, "I'm responsible for this and with God's help, I will do it!" They dive into their tasks and glorify God by their devotion to duty — not the success of the endeavor. Godly stewards don't dodge, ditch, or dump their responsibilities. They don't avoid being asked. They don't postpone, procrastinate, or point fingers — they desire to serve God! They care about others and their needs. No matter how hard the work, how stressful the resistance, or how unnoticed their effort, they never become un-Christlike doing the work of Christ. They don't trample others down in the name of productivity, meeting deadlines, and impressing others.

Godly stewardship is more a matter of attitude than it is action. Of course, if the attitude is right, the actions will take care of themselves. With the right attitude, actions become real acts of worship to God.

Mary did something really nice for Jesus. She took a pound of very expensive "genuine spikenard ointment," a luxurious perfume, and rubbed it over the feet of Jesus. It was an incredible act of unselfishness and love. The spikenard oil was worth the equivalent of one year's salary for the average person, and she'd been saving it for something special. The something became *someone,* and she freely used it to honor Him.

Judas, the bean counter of the group, argued that the money from the sale of the ointment could have helped a lot of poor people. Sounds reasonable — sounds like something a good steward would say. The problem is that Judas wasn't a good steward; he was a thief. Mary, who seemed to be wasting "three hundred denarii" worth of ointment, was the real good steward. Why? Because it was an act of compassion. Jesus knew that her heart was focused on glorifying God. Honoring Jesus is what good stewards do. She was a good steward in her heart, and it showed in her actions (John 12:1-8).

Mary displayed the attitude and actions of a godly steward, but most of all, she displayed the emptied-Himself mind of Christ. Not too long after this event, just one chapter later in John (13:1-17), Jesus took a towel and basin of water and washed His apostles' feet. This further reinforced the power of Mary's display of stewardship.

We can never go wrong if we use Jesus as our example of how to be good stewards in the sight of God. One of the most powerful descriptions of total stewardship is seen in that famous passage about the way Jesus grew and developed as a man. In Luke 2:52, right after relating the story of the twelve-year-old Jesus in the temple, the Bible says, "And Jesus kept increasing in wisdom and stature, and in favor with God and men."

This provides a good starting point for our own growth in stewardship. Jesus grew completely. He was a good steward of His mind, by growing in wisdom, and a good steward of His body, as He grew in stature. At the same time, His relationship with His Father continued to increase, and His sharing of that relationship with others wasn't an obstacle to His being favorably received by them.

If we are really ready to please God in every way we possibly can, we need to follow in the footsteps of Jesus. Our stewardship, like His, must be complete, consistent, and total. Stewardship of our minds means that we please

God with our minds. Like Jesus, we seek the favor of the Father.

THE JESUS OUTLINE

There are as many ideas and opinions about how to interpret the Bible as there are translations of it. Some are dogmatic in their opinions while others are more speculative. Some see a formula in Scripture for interpreting Scripture while others approach it from personal theories. I never have considered myself to be a scholarly theologian (please no loud "Amens"), but it has always seemed to me that God is very clear about what He wants. From Moses to Jesus to Paul, Peter, and James, He made it clear that He wants us to love Him with all our hearts, our souls, our minds, and our strength. Nearly everything He requires of us is clear: obedience, belief in His Son, godly living, and showing our love for Him by loving one another.

Some things fit into the category I call "Jigsaw Puzzle Theology." These are doctrinal conclusions that result from putting all the pieces of a theological conclusion together from bits and pieces found all over the Bible. They may not be wrong conclusions, but at the very least, we need to recognize that the important things of God are clear and simple. Not everyone, however, may be able to put all the pieces together, and very few of the millions and millions of people who have lived in the last two thousand years have had access to all the pieces. Unfortunately, these are the things that we spend most of our time arguing and dividing over.

"Jigsaw Puzzle Theology" may not be completely wrong, but we certainly ought to be more tolerant and understanding of others who haven't found all the pieces yet, and recognize that we may not have all the pieces or have them put together right ourselves.

101

Jesus addresses some difficult and complex subjects in His ministry, but He had a way of making them simple and understandable to the common people. In Matthew 25, Jesus gave a very clear and precise explanation for what constitutes good stewardship of our minds. He told three parables that spell out how we should think and act if we would please God.

The first parable is the parable of the ten maidens (vv. 1-13). It is a familiar story, but the summary is about ten maids of honor at a wedding. It was their job to carry lamps to light the scene when the bridegroom arrived. Five of them were wise, but the other five were foolish. They hadn't prepared for the event by making sure they had plenty of oil for their lamps. While they were gone trying to purchase some additional oil, the bridegroom arrived, took the five who were prepared into the wedding feast and shut the door. By the time the other five arrived, it was too late to get in.

While the obvious lesson is that we should be ready and prepared for the Bridegroom/Jesus when He comes, we have to ask ourselves, "Why weren't they ready?" We could speculate about the reasons or excuses, but the bottom line is that they were not motivated to be prepared.

To please God by being good stewards of our minds, we must first be motivated to do it.

In the second parable of Matthew 25, Jesus tells about a master who gives three of his servants certain responsibilities or talents to steward while he is gone. He gave one five talents, another two talents, and the final one just a single talent. When he returned and checked on their progress, the first two had doubled their respective talents. The one with the single talent, however, had buried his and thought the master would be pleased. He wasn't. It turned out that he was seriously out-of-touch with what his master wanted. His master condemned him, took his talent away, and cast him "into the outer darkness" (vv. 14-30).

The one-talent man was a "wicked, lazy slave" who squandered his master's gift. We usually say that he was condemned for not using his talent, but in reality, he was condemned for being irresponsible and untrustworthy.

To please God by being good stewards of our minds,
we must be responsible and trustworthy.

The final story is the Judgment scene (vv. 31-46). Jesus tells about all people being gathered together for Judgment. They are separated into two groups — the sheep and the goats, or the saved and the lost. The saved are honored for their service to those in need. They helped the hungry, the thirsty, the stranger, the naked, the sick, and the imprisoned. The lost are condemned for not helping the same group. They found out that when they refused to care or help, they were refusing Jesus as well as the people in need. Their choice resulted in their receiving eternal punishment while the saved received eternal life.

Again, the obvious lesson seems to be service, but it's the attitude that Jesus is most concerned about. Some cared for the needy while others ignored the needy. The attitude that was lacking for the lost and present for the saved was compassion. Jesus was constantly "moved with compassion" to help others. His servants, stewards of His will, can do no less.

To please God by being good stewards of our minds,
we must be compassionate and loving.

Let's briefly look at Jesus' three-point outline for being stewards of our minds.

MOTIVATED STEWARDS

You know what they say about fisherman stories? The first liar doesn't stand a chance. There is something about the telling of a fishing story that strains the ability of a person to stay objective. I like the story about the fisherman who strolled up to one of his fishing buddies and said, "Man, I caught a 250 pound marlin the other day!"

His buddy gave him one of those you-gotta-be-kidding-me looks, and said, "That's nothing. The other day when I was fishing, I hooked a lamp from an old Spanish ship. In fact, the lamp light was still lit!"

The marlin catcher lowered his head and replied, "Okay. If you'll blow out the light, I'll take 200 pounds off the marlin!"

The moral of that story is, truth is in the brain, but sometimes it takes special motivation to get it out.

God gave us our brains. He put all the cells and electrical impulses in place that allow us to think, reflect, conclude, and make choices. It's His and we must make sure that our minds please Him. Stewardship of our minds may be the hardest, but most important, responsibility we have as His stewards. In fact, at times we all wonder if we have any control at all over the gray matter between our ears.

The only truly private domain in your life is your mind. It is where the real "you" lives and where the real feelings are felt. We can fool everyone by pretending to be something we're not. Even the people who know and love us the most can be totally deceived about our true feelings. But — we know, and we know that God knows! The more we walk with God, the more our thought processes change from conversing with ourselves in our heads, to conversing with God, who is also in our heads/hearts.

I believe that the most miserable people in the world are the people who live lives of inconsistency between what they portray and what they really feel. That misery is compounded by the knowledge that the creator of heaven and earth knows about the inconsistency. He is the only one who can bring consistency into our life, and along with that, the peace that passes understanding.

Developing a mind that is pleasing to God begins with motivation. How badly do you want it? Do you truly crave a heart-level relationship with Him? Do you really want the peace of mind that comes from being open, honest, and totally consistent as you walk with Him? How much do you want it? Are you sick of sin and want the security of knowing that He paid your debt? How much do you want that *feeling*? Do you want a mind that is close to God — in communion with Him no matter where you are?

It's a struggle. Satan wants control of our minds, and he is willing to do whatever it takes to distract us from God. Paul described that very struggle in his own life in Romans 7:14-25. He shared his frustration over not being able to do the right things. He said, ". . . for I am not practicing what I *would* like to *do*, but I am doing the very thing I hate. . . . for the wishing is present in me, but the doing of the good is not. . . . But if I am doing the very thing I do not wish, I am no longer the one doing it, but sin which dwells in me." He described what was going on in his mind as "waging war" and "making me a prisoner." He reached a point where he could only cry out, "Wretched man that I am! Who will set me free from the body of this death?" (v. 24).

Truly wanting to please God is a big part of the battle. It is only won with the help of God. We must be motivated by love. As Paul said, "For the love of Christ controls us" (2 Cor 5:14). Once we have concluded that and committed to it, we adopt His mind-set (Phil 2:5), and we fill our minds with the things that please God. He wants us to dwell on things true, honorable, right, pure, lovely, of good repute, things excellent and worthy of praise. "Let your mind dwell on these things. The things you have learned and received and heard and seen in me, practice these things; and the God of peace shall be with you" (Phil 4:8-9).

To borrow a phrase from every football coach in the world, "You gotta want it!"

RESPONSIBLE STEWARDS

We've all heard the TV commercials for a specific college fund that warns, "A mind is a terrible thing to waste." To take that precious gift — that talent — and bury it in dirt, trash, or garbage is a sad way to use such an incredible God-given blessing. When the Master returns, and He will, He won't be pleased with the irresponsible handling of a mind that is wasted.

We are stewards of our minds. God entrusted us with the responsibility of filling them and using them to His glory and honor. He is trusting, and He has given us everything we need to live godly lives (2 Pet 1:3). If we ignore His trust in us and we ignore all the helpful tools He has given us, that may indicate our lack of trust in Him. Does He really want us to grow in Christ? Will He really help us? Is He really coming back to judge those who are disobedient? Yes, yes, and yes!

Sometimes we are like the elderly man in West Virginia who was taken on a plane ride for his birthday. He'd spent his whole life in that little town, never leaving it, and certainly never flying above it. After twenty minutes of circling the area and landing, one of the townsfolk asked, "Were you scared, Uncle Dudley?" "No-o-o," he responded in a shaky voice, "but I never did put my full weight down."[10]

You say that you trust God, but maybe you haven't put your full weight down on Him yet. Your faith and your commitment may be halfhearted. He left you with this great talent, and He's coming back sometime, and you're still thinking that burying it is an option. Some bury their minds in intellectualism and don't think there's room for God. Some bury their minds in selfishness and don't want to find room for God. Some even bury their minds in filth, pornography, and other worldly trash, and hope He's not returning anytime soon.

Anything that we put into our minds that cannot glorify God is something we don't need. Would you be comfortable having Jesus with you everywhere you go? Would He go into that establishment? Would He attend that movie, read that book, be around those people? There's a time for education and a time for entertainment, but there's never a time for God's people to be in the gutter unless they are rescuing someone.

Paul encouraged us to stay focused on spiritual things. In Colossians 3:1-17 is a series of pleas for us to be changed and to be new people because of having Jesus in our lives. As Christians, we must "keep seeking the things above, where Christ is, seated at the right hand of God. Set your mind on things above, not on the things that are on earth. For you have died and your life is hidden with Christ in God."

Our minds must stay focused on Jesus and His will. Our lives are "hidden" in Him, which means He envelops us and is sovereign over our minds. Because of the changes He has made in us, we "consider the members of [our] earthly body as dead to immorality, impurity, passion, evil desire, and greed, which amounts to idolatry. For it is on account of these things that the wrath of God will come." There are just some things that our minds can't participate in. We are responsible for keeping things like this out of our God-given brains.

Since everything we do, say, and think comes from our minds, it becomes our biggest responsibility as trustworthy stewards. In that sense, we are truly like the one-talent man in Jesus' parable. The mind is your one talent, and it's the one talent that will make everything else you do glorify God. When it is fed, nurtured, and focused on God, it will bear the fruit of the Spirit in your life like God wants. If you bury it, or even just try to maintain it, without any endeavors to grow spiritually, we will be as disobedient and as condemned as that one-talent man was.

For us, the challenge is much different than the commercial quote at the beginning of this section. Let's change it to fit our Master's challenge. "The mind of Christ is a terrible thing to waste."

COMPASSIONATE STEWARDS

Several years ago, the congregation with which I was working decided to expand their benevolence ministry by moving it to a separate, much larger building. The intent was to seriously enlarge the program and serve several hundred families each week. It was going to cost a lot of money to clear the note on the facility and remodel it for that particular ministry. It was a wonderful plan and a wonderful way to feed and clothe the needy of our community.

Needless to say, like anything new, there were those who strongly disapproved and were vociferous in their opposition. One of the loudest complaints went something like this, "We'll have all kinds of people who will be getting food and clothing who aren't really needy. They'll just be ripping off the church. I've seen it happen time and again!"

My deeply theological response was, "So what?" Since we can't possibly know the hearts of people, like Jesus could, our task is to be compassionate regardless of the worthiness of the recipient's intentions. When we allow the works of Satan to make us cynical and unmoved with compassion, he has won twice. First with the cheater, and second with the calloused Christian. The church's pantry is robbed, but that's not as terrible as having its spirit of benevolence robbed.

In Jesus' judgment scene in Matthew 25, He judged the compassion of His followers who in reality were giving to Him. The person who receives benevolence when they don't need it will answer to God. Their attitude has absolutely no bearing on the compassion of the givers.

STEWARDS OF OUR MINDS

We live in a time when it's almost unnatural to think compassionately. Satan has us all filled with fear and suspicion, and every stranger is a crook, a con, or a panhandler. We've all experienced or heard about churches being taken advantage of and ripped off by traveling con-artists. So we restrict our benevolence to members only or have dropped it all together.

Our minds will only be Christlike to the extent that we have a Christlike compassion in them. This is not optional for the steward of God who wants to please his Master. Compassion, or love, is the single quality rewarded or condemned by Jesus at the Judgment. It isn't one of the spiritual elements we need to work on someday — it's the essence of Jesus! If we allow the world or our own selfishness to block out compassion, we are removing the quality that separates "pretty good folks" from children of God.

It may be unnatural to think compassionately, but it is *spiritual* to think compassionately. The world may never understand it, but the good steward must think in terms of "What can I do for others?" and "How can I help?" We identify with the Good Samaritan not the priest and the Levite (Luke 10:30-37). Society tells us to avoid strangers in need, become numb to requests for help, and desensitize any feelings of compassion. Jesus showed us that we shouldn't listen to society. He had compassion on the sick, the hurting, the outcasts, and the sinners. He was "moved with compassion" at times when even His own apostles were surprised and insensitive to the needs. It is impossible to fully understand Jesus without understanding the spirit of compassion that drove Him. We can't be good stewards of our minds without having compassionate minds.

FOOD FOR THOUGHT

To please God with your mind, you must be motivated, responsible, and compassionate. These are the three qualities Jesus emphasized in Matthew 25, at the end of His earthly ministry, to prepare His disciples to be good stewards of His will. A spiritually healthy mind is not just a matter of cerebral gymnastics, but also of brain food. We must give our minds the proper exercise and the proper nutrition.

Have you ever heard of anyone eating too many vegetables? Have you ever heard about anyone being obese totally because of overeating vegetables? I'm sure somebody somewhere has, but I've never heard of it and I'm married to a registered and licensed nutritionist. It's hard to eat too much of what's good for you. We're not overweight because we munch carrots all day or peel and eat cucumbers for lunch. We like the big, juicy slabs of meat, the deep-fried stuff, and the sweet-loaded desserts. Even though we know it's killing us, we just can't get enough of it.

God gave us some incredibly healthy brain food. He calls it "the fruit of the Spirit" (Gal 5:22-23). It's food that we can't overindulge in! He says, "Go ahead – pig out!" This stuff will help us "crucify the flesh with its passions and desires" and give us the nourishment we need to "walk by the Spirit" (vv. 24-25). There is no such thing as gluttony when it comes to love, joy, peace, patience, kindness, goodness, faithfulness, gentleness, and self-control. Being stuffed with this stuff is stewardship and worship, because it glorifies God.

So go ahead – stuff yourself with His fruit – and glorify Him in the process!

DISCUSSION QUESTIONS

1. Why is godly stewardship more than just doing a good job?

2. Why is Jesus the best example of stewardship?

3. Why is motivation so important to being a good steward?

4. Should a Christian put something into his or her mind that doesn't glorify God? When and why?

5. What are some things that make it difficult today to be compassionate?

CHAPTER SEVEN
Stewards of Our Bodies

Archery and bow hunting are two fast-growing sports in America today. They are growing in popularity among all age groups and with both men and women. Shooting a bow and arrow accurately involves a lot of skill and determination. That is especially true when that skill is used to hunt wild animals. It's not just a matter of shooting accuracy, but of range estimation. Most bow hunters have to become not only accurate shooters, but they have to do two things extremely well. First, they have to be able to estimate distances accurately, and they have to know what their effective range is.

The real challenge of bow hunting is having to get so close to your target before you can attempt a shot. When you are that close, it is truly a chore not to be heard, smelled, or seen, especially as you attempt to pull your bow back to shoot. I have limited my shooting to a range of about twenty-five yards. I could take much longer shots, but I don't because my accuracy diminishes the farther out I shoot, and I want to take only "good" shots.

That's the point. No one else is around when it comes time to take a shot. No one would know if I took one that was too long. There are no laws that control distance limitations. I know what's right, I set the limits, and I choose to live by them. It's called self-control.

As we study what it means to be good stewards of our bodies, we will find ourselves coming back to the topic of self-control over and over again. The Bible says that Jesus grew "in wisdom and stature, and in favor with God and men" (Luke 2:52). The word "stature" is an older word for physical growth of the body. Jesus grew up physically. Just prior to this verse, Jesus was twelve years old, but He didn't stay twelve — He became a man. It was His responsibility to take care of Himself, to stay alive, so He could carry out the will of His Father.

Some of His growth was simply a matter of the genes He had been given. His height, the color of His eyes and hair, and the shape of His nose, were all determined by those genes. He had no say in it (unless He planned it out with God ahead of time).

There were plenty of other things for which He was totally responsible. Things that He was a steward of and in control of. He had to take care of His body, because it was a gift from God. We don't have a lot of details about His life for most of His thirty-three years, but we can be sure that He was a good steward of everything God gave Him. He set limits, He restrained Himself, and He used self-control. That is what a good steward must do.

If we don't set limits on ourselves, we do harm to our bodies and can even shorten our lives. Our bodies were given to us by God — not to abuse but to use for His honor and glory. If you abuse it, you may lose it. You could say that we violate the warranty if we don't do standard maintenance.

STEWARDS OF OUR BODIES

Writing these words is a 1951 model, slightly used, but still in good condition. There is high mileage and some abuse, mostly from periods of idleness, and occasionally the motor sputters and groans at start-up, put it does get cranking without staying cranky. There is a need for constant adjustments and tuning, but with the right fuel and a good driver, it still eats up the road.

Sometimes I feel more like an old jalopy than a temple, but God has blessed me with far more good health than bad. My body is the most obvious and most used gift I have from God. Every breath I take needs to be a reminder of His awesome love and graciousness. Next to the salvation of our souls, our mind and body is the most precious gift we have from God. It's amazing that it is so difficult to remember that and use it to glorify Him.

Your body is the one gift you can't escape. You need it to enjoy all the other things He has done for you. He wants you to take care of it. That's why He gave us such a strong instinctive urge to survive and take care of our basic needs. However, as I mentioned in an earlier chapter, our blessings can become problems. We are so blessed now that we left survival needs a long time ago. Now we can't decide upon a restaurant, which dessert we like best, and which diet will be the most painless. It's almost as if the more blessings we receive, the poorer job we do of being good stewards.

Being raised in an incredibly wealthy nation and living an affluent life-style has caused many people to worship the "feel-good" spirit rather than the God who gives everything to us. It is easy to see that spirit in drug addicts, alcoholics, and immoral people, but what about our own "feel-good" addictions, like food, tobacco, shopping, entertainment, couch-potato living, and self-imposed stress? These all destroy the body, ignore our basic responsibility to be good stewards of our bodies, and result in our failure to glorify God.

While the problem seems to be abuse, the real problem is much deeper. There is little or nothing said in Scripture about most of those problems. Yes, gluttony, drunkenness, and anxiety are in the Bible, but even then, it's the deeper problems that underlie the abuse with which God is concerned.

We want to be true worshipers of God, but worship is a life that glorifies God by being a good steward of all He has given. Our bodies are given as "living and holy sacrifices" to God. Our bodies belong to Him! They must glorify Him! Why is it so hard to be good stewards of our bodies?

UNGODLY SUBMISSION

The man was in a big hurry, running late, and totally stressed out. He came to an intersection just at the beginning of a circus parade. He was stuck and had to wait. A sign on the first wagon read, "Barney's Circus with Fifty Elephants," so he started counting elephants in order to know exactly when he could cross. When he counted to fifty, he floored the accelerator to cross the intersection. Unfortunately, he had miscounted and he ran smack into the last elephant and killed it.

Several days later he received a bill from the circus owner for two-hundred thousand dollars. He grabbed the phone, called him up, and demanded, "What's going on here? $200,000 for one lousy elephant! That's insane!"

The owner calmly answered, "It's true, you only hit and killed one elephant, but you pulled the tails out of forty-nine others!"

I use that old preacher's story to illustrate the effects of a chain reaction. Rarely do people ever wake up one morning and say, "I think I'll start abusing my body." I've also never heard of anyone who was dying of cancer or heart disease declaring to their family, "Yeah, this is happening just as I planned it years ago!" Either one of those comments would lead anyone who heard it to question the sanity of that person. We all know that many life-threatening health problems are the result of a lifetime of abuse and neglect. When we ignore the dangers of doing things that are bad for our bodies because we don't see the immediate results, we've started a chain reaction that will work its way through the entire parade of our lives, and like the elephants, get us in the end.

The church at Corinth had plenty of problems. One of the problems for which Paul really hammered them was taking a brother to court to be judged "before the unrighteous and not before the saints." That was not good for the church, and it did not show the spirit of Christ that should have dominated the situation. He challenged them with "Why not rather be wronged? Why not rather be defrauded?" It would be better to take a loss than cause the church to look bad in the eyes of the world (1 Cor 6:1-8).

Paul was arguing that Christians are different. We are changed people because of God's love and grace. If that difference is not seen and obvious, how do we appear different to the unsaved? He declared,

> Or do you not know that the unrighteous shall not inherit the kingdom of God? Do not be deceived; neither fornicators, nor idolaters, nor adulterers, nor effeminate, nor homosexuals, nor thieves, nor the covetous, nor drunkards, nor revilers, nor swindlers, shall inherit the kingdom of God. And such were some of you; but you were washed, but you were sanctified, but you were justified in the name of the Lord Jesus Christ, and in the Spirit of our God (vv. 9-11).

This is a spiritual chain reaction. At one time, they were lost in sin — guilty of terrible violations of God's will. But they were washed by the blood of Jesus, set apart for holy service to God, and by the name of Jesus they were declared justified or free from condemnation. His point should have been obvious to them (and us). God has been so gracious to you — how could you not want to please Him in every way you possibly can?

It is in that context and because of that truth that Paul encourages them to remember that their bodies belong to God. This is the argument for totality and consistency again. If our goal is to honor God with everything He's given us, it must include our bodies too. We must not take something that belongs to God and should honor God, and then participate in immorality or anything else that is ungodly. So the first thing he deals with is the subject of submission.

> All things are lawful for me, but not all things are profitable. All things are lawful for me, but I will not be mastered by anything. Food is for the stomach, and the stomach is for food; but God will do away with both of them. Yet the body is not for immorality, but for the Lord; and the Lord is for the body (vv. 12-13).

It seems to me that the men and women in the early church reveled in their newfound liberty. This is a major theme throughout the first Corinthian letter. They enjoyed their freedom from the Law, with all its restrictions and requirements. They enjoyed their freedom from ritualism, traditionalism, and judgmental religion. They were free to speak, participate, and enjoy being children of God. They were free to use their spiritual gifts to edify one another (14:26). Women were free, for the first time, to participate in what had been essentially a male-dominated religion (11:5). They were free to think of everything they did as glorifying God (10:31). They were free to do things and eat things that had always been unlawful and unauthorized for faithful followers of God.

Paul teaches them a simple lesson. Freedom in Christ means using godly restraint. Having the right to do something doesn't mean it ought to be done. The law may allow you to take a brother to court, but is that the best way to glorify God and His church? One may have the right to eat a steak that came from a cow sacrificed to an idol, but if it sets a bad example, leads a weaker brother to violate his conscience, or promotes something ungodly, it needs to be avoided. The personal right is subordinated for the needs of others and to the glory of God. What is lawful or allowable must be examined under the lens of "profitability." Is it what's best for God, for others, and lastly for myself?

Later in his letter, Paul uses the exact same comment to bring the eating of meat that had been offered to idols into perspective for us. They had taken their freedom a little too far. So he said again, "All things are lawful, but not all things are profitable." As further explanation he added, "All things are lawful, but not all things edify. Let no one seek his own *good*, but that of his neighbor" (10:23-24).

The point is the same as in 1 Corinthians chapter 6. There are things more important than your physical rights. Sometimes we need to be careful of a weaker brother, and other times we need to consider the reflection that it makes on the Lord's church. In chapter 6, Paul is also making an argument for being good stewards. We might think, "Well it's my life and my body; I'll do with it as I please!" Paul is declaring that logic spiritually illogical. He has already pointed out that they (we) were "washed," "sanctified," and "justified" by Jesus and the Holy Spirit. That means we need to realize that "me, mine, and ours" are now His!

Since I don't belong to me anymore, I need to make sure that what I do to me is profitable and edifies others. Not only must I take care of me, but I must not turn me over to anyone else or anything else. I can't allow myself to "be mastered by anything." Jesus must be the only Master of my life, my body, and my thoughts. To replace Him, even unintentionally, is idolatry.

All food was made by God. He gave us the need and desire for it, and the ability to appreciate and enjoy it. One of the great joys of living in prosperous times and in a country of plenty is lots of good food. We have more food than any other nation in the world, and we eat out more than any other people in the world. It should not be a surprise to discover that we have more overweight people than any other nation. We have more severely obese people, more weight-related health problems, and a higher percentage of people dieting than any other country in the world. That is amazing in view of the number of people around the world who go to bed hungry each night.

Food is not the problem. Paul said that all food and all of our stomachs will eventually be done away with (1 Cor 6:13). We must not be mastered by anything – including food! As good stewards of our bodies, we must control food and use it with moderation and never let it control us. The Corinthians were saying that food and the stomach were just natural things and have no connection to morality (or right or wrong). Paul points out that, while they are good and natural in and of themselves, they can become sinful if we let them control us.

Evidently they were making the same argument about promiscuous sex. They argued that it was merely a physical activity, like eating food, and it didn't have any bearing on one's spiritual life. Paul denies this line of thinking. God intended for food to be used for the body. The body needs it. But the body was not made or intended for immorality. The body was made to glorify God.[11]

The real issue is who's in charge. Jesus said that we can only have one master (Matt 6:24). If we let fleshly desires control us, whether it's the pull of the refrigerator or the pull of lust, then He's not the master of our lives. We can't submit ourselves to ungodly activities, even if those activities were godly in their origins. God gave us food, but not for us to submit to it and be controlled by it. God gave us sexual desires to be fulfilled in marriage, not through promiscuous behavior. Our bodies were not given to us by God for ungodly submission.

UNGODLY MEMBERSHIP

Between my junior and senior years in high school, I attempted to get a summer job with the government agency my mother worked for in Washington, D.C. It was a daunting task. It was the late sixties and the agency my mother worked for was the Central Intelligence Agency. It is probably safe to say that they were the most paranoid agency in America at that time, even more than the FBI because of the Cold War being in full swing.

The application was as thick as my English Grammar Workbook. It took me hours to fill out the entire thing. I still remember one of the final questions on the application. They asked if I was or had been a member of any of the organizations listed on an attached sheet. I pulled out the sheet — I mean sheets, and looked at it. It was several pages with three columns of lists on each page. The print was tiny too. It was obvious that this was a list of unacceptable organizations that would instantly remove my name from consideration if I happened to be or have been a part of any one of them.

It was an amazing list. I saw many that I recognized as subversive or un-American — at least by the conservatives who were in charge. Groups like the Students for a Democratic Society, the KKK, the Black Panthers, the SLN, and the Communist Party. There were a lot of organizations that I didn't recognize and several that surprised me by their inclusion. It really scared me to discover that there were so many organizations that our government found threatening. I was afraid to tell them that I'd been a Boy Scout and a member of the Beta Club.

Since then I have always been a little gun-shy about being associated with any group or organization that I did not completely understand and agree with. Who knows? I might want to quit preaching and become a CIA agent some day! Actually, I don't want to be part of anything that Jesus won't be part of. As a steward of God, I don't want to be part of anything ungodly.

Paul makes this same argument as he tries to convince the Corinthians, and us, that our bodies belong to God. He asked a question and then answered it himself.

> Now God has not only raised the Lord, but will also raise us up through His power. Do you not know that your bodies are members of Christ? Shall I then take away the members of Christ and make them members of a harlot? May it never be! Or do you not know that the one who joins himself to a harlot is one body *with her*? For He says, "The two will become one flesh." But the one who joins himself to the Lord is one spirit *with Him*. Flee immorality (1 Cor. 6:14-18a).

There is not a more important event in the history of mankind than the resurrection of Jesus. It confirmed His Messiahship, it was the cornerstone for God's redemption of man, and it became the proof for His return and our own resurrection. In the first gospel sermon, Peter told the assembled crowd, it happened, it's a fact, we saw it, now what are you going to do about it? (Acts 2:14-38). Every person who becomes a Christian has a strong faith in the reality of the resurrection of Jesus and what it means about our own resurrection.

Paul simply reaffirms that reality and that promise. Just as surely as Jesus was raised up from the dead by the power of God, you and I will be raised up by that same power. It may seem like he has changed subjects, but he hasn't. Paul is arguing for allegiance, loyalty, and indebtedness.

God is so good to us and He has done so much to secure our salvation, how could we possibly give our allegiance to anyone else? Jesus took our beating, our humiliation, our crown of thorns, carried our cross, and took our nails in His hands and feet. How could we even dream of betraying Him?

Our "bodies are members of Christ!" In the family of God there is no such thing as split allegiance. We are all either members of Christ or members of Satan. We can't say that our hearts belong to Jesus but our bodies belong to sin. Such inconsistency is ungodly. Paul discusses the inconsistency of saying that your body belongs to Jesus and at the same time using it to participate in immorality. Some of the Corinthians thought they could separate the things of the flesh and the things of the Spirit into two distinct areas of their life. They really thought that they could participate in immoral behavior and still consider themselves members of Christ. When we join ourselves to the Lord, we cancel all other memberships that are not in accord with His will. We become "one spirit with Him."

We want to be good stewards of our bodies because we want to please God and follow the example of Jesus. As mentioned before, asking ourselves what Jesus would do needs to become part of our lifestyle. In regards to what to do with our bodies, we really don't have much trouble trying to figure out what He would do. Would Jesus over-eat and be gluttonous? Would Jesus use tobacco, drugs, or become a drunkard? He would talk to a prostitute, not to solicit sex, but to offer "living water" that He would gladly give. Would He do anything that would conflict with His "membership" with God the Father? Would He do anything that didn't glorify His Father?

We know the answers to all those questions without having to think much at all. We also know how to be good stewards of our bodies without having to think too much. It's when we don't think like we should that we allow ourselves to be "mastered" by our physical desires and forget to whom we belong.

123

Our bodies are "members of Christ." That means we must please Him with our bodies, as good stewards, and that is part of what it means to be a "living and holy sacrifice" acceptable to God.

UNGODLY OWNERSHIP

Why do so many people abuse their bodies? So many harm their bodies by overeating and becoming overweight. About a fourth of the adult population put their lives at risk by smoking or using tobacco in some form. An even larger number of us lead sedentary lives and don't get the exercise that our bodies so desperately need to stay healthy and live longer. It is easy to condemn those who are addicted to drugs or alcohol because they are not socially acceptable, but far more of us will die from abusing and neglecting our bodies than those who overdose on illegal substances or destroy their livers with booze.

We all know that these problems often stem from poor self-control and poor self-esteem, but sometimes they come from pure old-fashioned thoughtlessness. Time and bad habits just catch up with us, and we end up suffering from the law of sowing and reaping.

Having said that, I need to point out that the other extreme is just as bad. Today many people are worshiping health food, exercise, and having beautiful bodies, not because they are good stewards, but because of pride and egotism. How many times have you heard some celebrity hawking a book or new exercise equipment proclaim, "Our bodies are our temples. You will feel so good about yourself when you look good!" So millions of people are jogging, lifting weights, and joining health clubs to "feel good about themselves," and to look like "one of the beautiful people."

Poor self-control is bad, but self-centeredness is worse. God can work with the weak (2 Cor 12:10), but He is "opposed to the proud" (Jas 4:6). As important as good health is, to focus on it — to worship one's body — is vain and prideful. Our bodies are neither temples to be worshiped nor are they objects intended to allow us to glorify ourselves. Paul said,

> Or do you not know that your body is a temple of the Holy Spirit who is in you, whom you have from God, and that you are not your own? For you have been bought with a price: therefore glorify God in your body (1 Cor 6:19-20).

We are stewards of our bodies, but God is interested in interior not exterior decorating. Being a temple of the Holy Spirit is not an excuse to focus on the physical or to seek the attention of man. The body is a temple of the Holy Spirit only in the sense that the Holy Spirit resides in us, not in the sense that the Holy Spirit needs a temple-like dwelling.

I believe that this is a literal passage. The Holy Spirit does literally dwell in us. I don't understand all of it and I don't believe it includes tingly feelings going up and down our spines or our hearing still voices in the night. The Bible says He is in us, and that's all I need (Acts 2:38). I don't believe this passage is teaching anything beyond good stewardship of our bodies, especially as we recognize that God's body, our body, cannot and must not be defiled by immorality.

I have heard many preachers and teachers misuse this passage or at least come close to it, as they used it to preach healthy living and how sinful it is to do anything unhealthy. They often left those with physical challenges and natural health problems feeling like sinners and broken temples. I used to get especially frustrated with overweight preachers preaching against the sin of smoking. I couldn't figure out how they made the distinction between destroying one's self with tobacco or obesity. One could always be an elder or minister and be overweight, but tobacco instantly disqualified anyone from either position. What's wrong with one is wrong with the other.

The temple was a holy place, a place where God was, and a place to communicate with Him. That is one of the great changes between the Old and New Covenants. We are the temple of God now, not some facility or cathedral somewhere. Each one of us is a priest with direct, personal access to God (1 Pet 2:9). We are each the offering or sacrifice (Rom. 12:1) and we are all living, breathing worship to God. Paul used the analogy of our bodies being a temple to emphasize our call to holiness and our responsibility to make sure our bodies glorify God.

The real point of the passage is *ownership*. Paul said, "You are not your own . . . you have been bought with a price." That may sound un-American, but then we are Christians first and Americans second. Jesus purchased our redemption with His blood. We belong to Him. Our bodies are not ours just to do with as we please or just to do what feels good. They belong to Him, so we must take care of them, but we must not let the gift replace the Giver in terms of what we worship. Our bodies are owned by Jesus, but that doesn't necessarily mean that having a healthy body is the top priority. If it were, why did God allow Paul to have so many hardships and physical struggles? Why did God send or allow Paul to have a "thorn in the flesh" if physical fitness was so important?

That's not to say it's unimportant, but it does teach us that He is more interested in our spiritual hearts than He is our physical health. There must be a balance somewhere. Paul gives that balance to us by declaring that you must "glorify God in your body." Whatever we do to our bodies, it must glorify God. If it doesn't glorify God — which abuse, gluttony, addiction, and neglect never do — then we should change our lifestyles so that we can.

We've had an entire chapter on glorifying God, but let's remember what "glorify" means. It means to reflect positively. When we glorify God, we do things that reflect positively on Him. We don't care about impressing man, inflating self, or copying the world. We care about making it clear that we belong to God, and that our bodies don't do anything to detract from that commitment.

In many respects, our bodies are just like singing, praying, studying the Word, breaking bread, and assembling together. They are all tools given by God to help us grow and serve Him. When used for the purpose He intended, we are obedient stewards, and He is worshiped and glorified.

Every now and then there is a short story on the evening news about a "good citizen" who found a large sum of money and then returned it to the owner. It's usually used as filler toward the end of the program because "good news" doesn't rate "top story" status. There was one such story on the other day, and the interviewer asked the man why he didn't just keep the money he'd found. The guy looked at the newscaster like he'd asked a stupid question, and he said, "I couldn't do that. It wasn't mine to keep. It belonged to someone else!" To him, it was that simple and that obvious.

He was not only a person with values and integrity, but he understood ownership. When we are pulled by the lure of what "feels good" and what might be "a lot of fun," we need to remember that simple and obvious solution. "I can't do that. This body isn't mine. It belongs to someone else."

As good as exercise is in helping us have healthy bodies, Paul said it is "only of little profit." That didn't mean that it was worthless, just not *as important* as applying that same effort and self-control to drawing closer to God. He said, ". . . godliness is profitable for all things, since it holds promise for the present life and *also* for the *life* to come" (1 Tim. 4:8). That doesn't mean that we ignore "bodily discipline" or exercise and good health. It simply means that we understand where real quality of life and the hope of eternal life come from. Focusing on the body is focusing on ourselves. Paul said, "We have fixed our hope on the living God, who is the Savior of all men" (v. 10). We need to be good stewards of our bodies, but it's far more important to be good stewards of our soul.

Even though we must be good stewards of our bodies, there are other things more important than protecting and preserving them. Jesus said that the greatest kind of love there is is to give one's life for a friend (John 15:13). Paul pointed out that if we give up our bodies to be burned, it is only profitable if it's done in love (1 Cor 13:3). Both of these passages describe what Jesus, the ultimate good steward, did for us. He loved us, and gave His body up to die on a cross as a replacement for our own punishment for sin.

Jesus took care of Himself, but He didn't focus on Himself. He lived to do the will of His Father. He wasn't anti food either. The Gospels are full of fellowship meals, dinners, and feasts. He fed thousands Himself. But we must remember, He ate to live, He didn't live to eat. He didn't push health, but He did condemn excesses, like gluttony and being a drunkard. Would He have ever done something that was bad for His body? He will always be the supreme example for us, so if we can't imagine Him doing something or being somewhere, then we should change and do what He would do.

We must be in submission to Him, remember that our bodies are members with Him, and never allow anything to confuse or detract from the fact that He owns us.

DISCUSSION QUESTIONS

1. Why is it true that the more blessings we receive the poorer job we do of being good stewards?

2. Why must Christians never let anything control their bodies?

3. Why can't a Christian say, "My heart belongs to Jesus, but my body belongs to sin?"

4. Paul said that our bodies are temples of the Holy Spirit. Is that a temple to be worshiped or a temple to be protected?

5. Jesus sacrificed His body for us. What does that tell us about being good stewards of our bodies?

CHAPTER EIGHT
Stewards of Our Souls

The Mess Hall needed a new roof. This particular Mess Hall held a lot of special memories for me. It was in the middle of Camp Wamava, which was in the middle of the spectacular Blue Ridge Mountains. Camp Wamava was a church camp that I started attending when I was about ten years old. It was my oasis from the mean streets of Washington, D.C. where we lived. Before the Interstates were put in, it used to take us about an hour and a half to make the drive up to camp to drop me off. The first summer I attended, I'd signed up for one week. After I'd been there a few days, I ended up adding on another three weeks. I spent the better part of every summer up in those lush green mountains with their cool mornings and star-filled nights.

Through the years I moved from being a camper to a Junior Staffer, and finally on to being a Senior Staffer. The summer after I graduated from High School, I spent ten

weeks at camp. For two weeks I helped build a new bar-
racks, and then became the Recreation Director for the
entire eight weeks of summer camp. It capped off about
ten years of attending camp. Seven years later, my wife and
I and our six-month-old daughter Deborah, moved to
Northern Virginia to work with a church in the Washington, D.C. suburbs. I returned to camp occasionally to teach
a Bible class for a week, and we had several youth and
men's retreats at the facility. I also obtained permission to
hunt on the land next to camp, which gave me plenty of
reasons to be back in those special mountains as often as I
could.

About three years into that ministry, one of the camp
board members asked me if I'd consider helping him put a
new roof on the old camp Mess Hall. Once I'd committed
to help, the "we" became "me," and I found myself up on
the roof, in the mountains, destroying the peace and seren-
ity as I hammered nails into roofing shingles. If I had to do
manual labor, that was the perfect place to do it.

It was a huge roof and I spent many hours hauling bun-
dles of roofing shingles up the ladder and nailing them
down in perfectly measured rows. Between hammer blows,
the peace and quiet of nature ruled. Many times I had to just
stop and enjoy the beauty that surrounded me. On several
occasions, deer would stroll out and feed on the softball
field in the valley just below the Mess Hall. I wasn't being
lazy, I just had to stop and enjoy their presence for a while.

The greatest joy of the job came when the board
member came up to see the finished work. He looked it
over carefully, checking the ridge lines, the straightness of
the rows, and the closeness of each seam. After the exami-
nation, he turned to me and said, "You did a good job."

It wasn't a huge commendation, but it was all I had
been looking for, and I felt really good. There's something
very fulfilling about having been entrusted with a job and
having it declared "good."

That roof was nothing compared to what God has entrusted into my care. Everything I have has been given to me by God, and I am responsible for being a good steward of every bit of it. This is total stewardship, just as my worship is my total life. Everything must glorify Him — if I am interested in pleasing Him — and I am.

Jesus grew in wisdom and stature, which is mind and body, and He also grew in favor with God (Luke 2:52). Since God is concerned with our hearts, hearts that love Him completely, the way to grow in His favor is to focus on matters of the soul. I must be a good steward of my soul. My mind and body only have meaning as tools to please God when I make sure that my soul is firmly in His hands.

This may sound very abstract and theoretical, but that is where the real battle takes place. Peter warned, "Abstain from fleshly lusts, which wage war against the soul" (1 Pet 2:11). It may seem like the fight is only a matter of controlling the mind and the body, but it is our soul that Satan is really after. This passage makes it clear that we cannot separate "fleshly lusts" from spiritual consequences. Notice that he didn't say "fleshly practices," which are obviously sin, but rather "fleshly lusts." The mind that dwells on fleshly desires gradually chips away the presence of the Spirit in our hearts. It may not seem as dangerous, because we feel like we haven't really committed an immoral act, but the mind can hold a lot more pollution than the body can participate in.

John expanded this when he said, "For all that is in the world, the lust of the flesh and the lust of the eyes and the boastful pride of life, is not from the Father, but is from the world" (1 John 2:16). All three of these wage war on the soul. A mind that is full of lust and pride is a mind that has pushed God out and placed one's soul in jeopardy. That is why we are encouraged over and over again in the Word to fill our minds with spiritually nutritious food that will bring us closer to God. Paul even gave us a sample list that included, "whatever is true, whatever is honorable, whatever is right, whatever is pure, whatever is lovely, whatever is of good repute, if there is any excellence and if anything worthy of praise, let your mind dwell on these things" (Phil 4:8). He also pointed out that the fruit of the Spirit, in Galatians 5:22-23, is really excellent soul food.

The Bible is our owner's manual for how we are to take care of our souls. It is filled with guidance, exhortations, warnings, and instructions. Most of all, it tells us about the Master Steward, Jesus, and how He walked this earth and did nothing to displease His Father. If we are going to be good stewards of our souls, we must pay close attention to His will and do the things that will protect our souls.

There are three simple and very practical observations that I want to make that will help us do the job. I call them **Principles of Soul Protection.**

THE FEAR PRINCIPLE

She was filled with fear. She'd been single so long that her picture was used in the dictionary to define "spinster." What she was fearful of was that her new boyfriend, one she finally felt would "pop the question" any day, would find out about her failing eyesight. She devised a plan to keep him from noticing her condition. She went out into the forest where they usually took their walks, and stuck a pin in a tree. The next day, as they were strolling towards the forest, she suddenly stopped, pointed in the right direction, and said, "Isn't that a pin sticking in that tree way over there?" As she ran to retrieve it, she tripped over a cow.

Fear will make us do some strange things. We live with locks, latches, and security systems. We don't go out at night. We refuse to do anything that requires us to stand

134

up in front of a crowd. We don't try or even consider doing some things because we fear failing, we fear rejection, and we fear ridicule. The list is endless.

Many times, fear is appropriate and good. It keeps us from breaking traffic laws, cheating on our taxes, and shooting the neighbor's barking dog. Sometimes fear is more than good, it is essential.

Solomon, the King who was so wise that he had to find out for himself that worldly pursuits are a waste of time, concluded that our whole purpose for existing was to "fear God and keep His commandments because . . . God will bring every act to judgment, everything which is hidden, whether it is good or evil" (Eccl. 12:13-14). He put it another way in Proverbs 1:7, when he said, "The fear of the LORD is the beginning of knowledge."

Any persons who consider themselves knowledgeable must have a fear of the Lord or their mental capabilities are questionable. Everything significant must begin with a healthy fear of God. Without it, there is no foundation, no starting point, and no truth. If one doesn't begin with a fear of God, there is only theory, speculation, and hypothesis to work with.

The fear of the Lord is where our relationship with Him must begin. We are like the two-year-old who doesn't understand electricity. All the two-year-old understands is that he had better not play with the electrical outlet or Mommy and Daddy will get really upset and punish him. Like that child, our relationship must include fear, respect, power, and the certainty of punishment. Because God is real, our accountability is certain. And since His wrath or blessings are based on truths and absolutes, we never lose that sense of fear, but we do move beyond it to something higher and more spiritual.

God wants our love, but He demands our fear. He requires every person to recognize that we have a soul, and it is our responsibility to be good stewards of that soul.

Fear will always bring us back to that higher priority. It's not a matter of "if" we will answer for our souls, but "when." Whether it is at the instance of death or at the return of Jesus, it will happen.

Our struggle as stewards is essentially twofold. We move from fear, though never totally, in our relationship with God to love. And secondly, we must not let this world's fears have a higher priority than the fear we are to have for God.

The first epistle of John is almost completely focused on our need to grow in love for God. Love is how we know we belong to Him, it shows us that we abide in Him, it is the natural response to His love, it is being like Him, it makes us complete, it gives us confidence in Him and our salvation, it is the true test of consistency and discipleship, and it "casts out fear" (1 John 4:7-21). Bottom line? It's how we, as good stewards of our souls, secure our souls.

The problem is not letting life's fears supersede or distract us from fearing God. Sometimes we let our fear of rejection and ridicule by others become a higher priority than our obedience to God. We want to be accepted, to fit in, and not to be seen as some crazy fanatic. So we learn to blend, to conform, and to be acceptable. That is not always wrong. Paul talked about fitting in when he said, "I have become all things to all men, that I may by all means save some" (1 Cor 9:22). He was not talking about trying to fit in so that he would feel good about himself because he was accepted. He was talking about trying to fit in so that he could have an opportunity to share Jesus with people. His confidence and self-esteem came from God not man. You only have to read his list of sufferings in 2 Corinthians 11 to discover how often he was unacceptable to man.

He is the same person who told us to "not be conformed to this world, but be transformed by the renewing of your mind" (Rom 12:2). Trying to evangelize from the inside of a group is not the same thing as adopting their worldview. While we may appear to be "one of the group," we have a higher responsibility to our souls to "prove what the will of God is, that which is good and acceptable and perfect." We never stop desiring to be acceptable to God.

Sometimes our fear of physical harm paralyzes our desire to do His will. No sane person wants to be hurt or lose his life, but we must never let even that overshadow the greater fear we must have for God.

Jesus was trying to get His disciples ready for the hardships that were ahead of them. He pointed out to them that a disciple can usually plan on being accepted and treated just like the Master was. If He was ridiculed and rejected, shouldn't His disciples expect the same?

He admonished them to remember the higher priority. He said, "And do not fear those who kill the body, but are unable to kill the soul; but rather fear Him who is able to destroy both soul and body in hell" (Matt 10:24-28).

All man can possibly do is destroy our bodies. We knew all along that our bodies were only temporary anyway! We can't get to heaven with these old vessels of flesh and bone. If man takes that away, we just get to be with God and Jesus a little sooner. The true test of overcoming the flesh is when we can truly say as Paul did, "For to me, to live is Christ, and to die is gain" (Phil 1:21).

Is it really a gain? Do we believe that? Is it really that hard to want to go to a place with no pain, sickness, death, or tears? Is it really difficult to want to escape the fire of Hell, especially when we know we deserve it? Is there any pleasure on earth that can possibly match the joy of Heaven? How can a few years on this planet compare to eternity with all the saints, Jesus, and God?

The Fear Principle simply helps us remember the preeminence of the soul over the flesh. We must be good stewards of both, but ultimately only one goes to be with the Father.

THE FLEE PRINCIPLE

You've probably heard sermons about all the "lettuce" verses in the Bible. It's a play on words about the "let us" passages. Then there is the "tater" sermon about all the "taters" in the church. You know, the spec-taters, and the agi-taters, and such like. It is such an old play on words, that they didn't get to use the new one — couch po-taters.

I remember hearing a sermon many years ago about "The Fleas in the Bible." It turned out to be about all the passages that called on us to "flee" something. I personally love puns and any kind of wordplay, but this is really serious business. Our souls are so important, and our responsibility to protect them is so great, when it comes to things that might harm our souls, as the old country boy says, "Sometimes you just gotta run away from it!"

In the mid-eighties I went on a bow hunting trip to Alaska. We were hunting for caribou. A floatplane dropped us off on the shores of a small lake in the middle of nowhere, and flew off leaving my partner and me totally alone. We received a lot of advice about what to do if we ran into one of Alaska's giant grizzlies. Everything from "pray" to "shoot yourself." The one thing that everyone told us was, don't try to run away from one. It triggers their attack response, and they run thirty-five miles an hour, so you'll never get away.

That sounded reasonable, until we saw our first grizzly. It was eight and a half feet long/tall, and probably weighed close to half a ton. It was about a half mile away from us, but that was plenty close for me. The next day we found some huge grizzly tracks within fifty feet of our tent. One had checked us out at night and decided not to crash our party.

I'm sorry, but even with all the warnings, if I had one of those gigantic meat eaters coming at me, I'd do my best to make sure it choked to death on my trail dust. I'd run like a wild man. Wisdom may say stand still, but every fiber of my body would say, "Run! Forget standing still!"

It is just the opposite when it comes to dealing with temptations. Sometimes we can't just stand still and hope it goes away. There are temptations that are so alluring and dangerous to our souls that we must run away as fast and as far as we can.

Joseph didn't spend much time debating with Potiphar's wife when she tried to force him to commit sin with her. In the past, she had tried to talk him into sinning with her, but he simply refused and got on with his work. But when she became aggressive, he exited the scene as fast as his legs could carry him. Even though she lied about what happened, and caused Joseph to go to prison, he honored God, protected his soul, and was able to be used by God for great things in the future (Genesis 39).

"Sometimes you just gotta run!" To protect our souls, sometimes the only wise course of action is to remove ourselves from the temptation. Paul said, "Flee fornication!" (1 Cor 6:18). That means don't mess around or see how close you can get to the sin! Run from it!

Paul said the same thing about idolatry. He declared in 1 Corinthians 10:14, "Flee idolatry." The context of the passage is referring to Israel's nasty habit of forgetting God and letting themselves get pulled into the idolatry of their neighbors. Paul commands us to run from it. Don't let it have any pull on you at all! This is especially important as we remember that some idols are not as obvious as others. Some may be statues or shrines, but others may be careers and things that come before God. Those strange little pieces of paper with pictures of presidents on them have a way of becoming idols. Run!

Paul made a more sweeping use of the warning to "flee" when he said, "Flee youthful passions" (2 Tim 2:22). The younger you are, the more you tend to feel invincible when it comes to withstanding temptations. It's wonderful that they feel confident enough to say, "I can handle it," but the reality is that they usually can't. They don't have the experience to see where things will lead. That's why parents worry so much about their kids. It's hard to teach them to run from something that they don't see as a threat. Yet, so often that is the very best thing they could do. Temptations are powerful tools of Satan. Young people (and older people) need to understand: don't play with it, toy with it, get close to it, or underrate its power to destroy. Run! You will never regret running from something that could harm your soul.

We are born with the automatic instinct to protect ourselves through fleeing or fighting. It's called the "Fight or Flight Instinct." Our mind instantly evaluates the danger and sends impulses all through the body to run, or get ready to fight. That is not just a physical instinct, it is also a spiritual reaction. There are times when we must "fight the good fight of faith" (1 Tim 6:12) and as James declares, "Resist the devil and he will flee" (Jas 4:7). It's nice to put him on the defensive occasionally. That is not only an admonition, but a promise. If we resist the devil — truly fight back and refuse his influence, he will leave us at that moment. He'll come back and be ready for another fight, but he will respect his rejection.

Other times, it's our turn to flee. Run — don't let lust get a grip on you. Run from pride, because it feels so natural to inflate your own ego. Run from materialism, greed, covetousness, and the love of money. They're dangerous, insidious, and dominating. Your soul is too valuable to be sold out to one of Satan's tricks.

Protect your soul with all your might. It was purchased at an incredible cost, and the One who paid that price wants you with Him for all eternity.

So run whenever you have to. Where are you going to run to? The Psalmist said, "O LORD . . . I flee unto Thee to hide me" (Ps. 143:9, KJV). Run into the arms of God, and He'll protect your soul.

THE FOCUS PRINCIPLE

Every child of God needs to develop what the old farmer called "plow eyes." In farming, that is the ability to stay focused on where you are going with the plow. If you don't keep your eyes looking forward, at that distant point where the furrow is to finish, you are likely to wander all over and have crooked furrows.

I've never plowed a field, but I have mowed some pretty big yards. On the first cutting trip, if you don't stay focused on the point you are going to, the row you cut will not be straight, and it will throw off all the following rows. Rather than having a neatly cut yard, the neighbors will be wondering about your level of sobriety.

Jesus seems to have had some "fair weather" followers during His ministry who loved to look like they were His disciples, but lacked the commitment necessary to remain faithful. He asked some of them to make a commitment, and they all had an excuse for why they couldn't at that time. Jesus didn't pull any punches when He responded to their lack of dedication. He said, "No one, after putting his hand to the plow and looking back, is fit for the kingdom of God" (Luke 9:57-62).

Jesus wants disciples with "plow eyes" — disciples who can stay focused on the mission given to them by the Father. He understood that when He was just twelve years old and His parents "found Him in the temple, sitting in the midst of the teachers, both listening to them, and asking them questions." Everyone who saw this was amazed by His wisdom and maturity. His mother, however, was more interested in finding out why He had disappeared and not stayed with their group. His literal response was that He had to be "in the things or affairs of My Father." It was time for Him, even at such a young age, to focus on His Father's mission for Him (Luke 2:46-49).

A good steward must stay focused on the task given by the Master. Each one of us will stand before God and give account of our stewardship. We must understand that "I forgot" is not an acceptable excuse. A steward lives for the Master! To say, "Your will just slipped my mind" is a confession of apathy and disobedience. There is nothing more important than His will and there is nothing that must be allowed to distract us from His will.

Paul encouraged us to "Let the word of Christ richly dwell within you" (Col 3:16). That is a loving way of telling us to stay focused on His will. What the Master says is not idle conversation or meaningless jabber. It is the most powerful message ever shared! It is His plan for saving our souls, helping us to be good stewards, and giving us the mission to pass it on to others. The Hebrew writer said, "For the word of God is living and active and sharper than any two-edged sword, and piercing as far as the division of soul and spirit, of both joints and marrow, and able to judge the thoughts and intentions of the heart" (Heb 4:12). That is some powerful stuff! Too powerful to ignore, forget, or treat lightly. It's a loaded weapon that cuts to the soul and reveals what is really going on inside of us. If His word really does dwell in us and it is living and active, how can we be anything less than living and active stewards of His word?

Stewards stay focused on the Master's word/will, and like any submissive servant, we never take our eyes off of Him. Even in the world there is no difference between the master and the will of the master as far as the steward is concerned. But in the spiritual realm, it is even more true because Jesus and the Word, are one and the same (John 1:1). His word helps us know and understand Him, and makes us aware of His constant presence. Once we have grasped all that, we stay focused on Him in order to please Him and be like Him.

The Word says, "Let us run with endurance the race that

is set before us." To run a race, we have to know the course and where the finish line is. If we don't stay on a straight course, we could get lost. The Word gives us that direction and point of focus. It says, "fixing our eyes on Jesus, the author and perfecter of faith" (Heb 12:1-2). If we don't keep our focus on Him, we get side-tracked, or forgetful, or lose sight of how important our souls are. The best thing that we can do for our soul is to stay focused on Jesus and His Word.

One final thought about being good stewards of our souls: We need to be careful about being TOO focused on OUR souls. As mentioned, they belong to God and we are simply stewards of them. It's also important to remember that we get our greatest joy and spiritual blessings when we help others to be good stewards of their souls.

James ended his epistle with an interesting admonition and challenge. He said, "My brethren, if any among you strays from the truth, and one turns him back, let him know that he who turns a sinner from the error of his way will save his soul from death, and will cover a multitude of sins" (Jas 5:19-20).

We need to invest ourselves in others and help them stay focused. When we do, a soul is saved and a multitude of sins is covered. What's interesting about this passage is trying to determine who the recipient of the soul-saving and sin covering is. Is it the one turned back? That seems obvious and probable, but could it include the one doing the turning? Is it possible that grace was given to us to be shared with others so that more grace could be given back to us? That's problematic to say the least, but it's interesting that a letter to the early Christians, and to us, ended with such a powerful call for stewardship of the souls of others.

It may sound silly, but we need to remember that the main thing is to keep the main thing the main thing! What is the main thing? Saving souls — starting with our own!

The main thing isn't building buildings, installing the latest technology, or developing a relevant style in our assembly. These things aren't unimportant, they're just not the main thing, and sometimes they distract us from the main thing. We are in the soul-saving business — period! Everything we do from organizing to expenditures should either save souls or edify and equip souls.

Jesus' warning is not just for the worldly and un-churched heathens. He said, "For what will a man be profited, if he gains the whole world, and forfeits his soul? Or what will a man give in exchange for his soul?" (Matt 16:26). What have we gained if we have incredible buildings, dazzling audio-visual equipment, and a snappy, contemporary style of assembly, but we don't reach souls for Christ? Jesus' question should haunt us on a daily basis. "What will a man give in exchange for his soul?" What is more valuable than our soul? The obvious answer is absolutely nothing, yet many people have made the decision that Satan has a better idea. Many have cheapened the value of their soul by selling out to pleasure, selfishness, materialism, institutionalism, hypocrisy, greed, immorality, and self-righteousness — just to name a few.

If you get what you want, will you want what you get for eternity! I once heard Chuck Swindoll say, "I never saw a hearse pulling a U-Haul." We really can't take it with us because ultimately only our soul will last for eternity. There is nothing more valuable, more precious, and more important to a good steward of the gifts of God than our soul. The whole world will perish, but our soul will last forever. Make sure your forever is with God! Be a good steward of your soul!

DISCUSSION QUESTIONS

1. How do "fleshly lusts" wage war on the soul?

2. How important is fear in our relationship with God?

3. What are some examples when fleeing is the best way to deal with sin?

4. Why is focus so important in being a good steward of our soul?

5. As stewards of God, what is "the main thing?"

CHAPTER NINE
Stewards of Our Cross

The sun was shining bright and beautiful. As I sat comfortably in my car, protected from the wind and the cold, I temporarily forgot that it was winter. Then I stepped out of my car and received a sudden reminder as the biting wind seemed to cut right through my dark blue suit. Whoever invented men's suits, didn't invent them to keep you warm. Suits are one of society's uniforms and serve only to make us acceptable to others who expect us to wear them.

This was my official funeral suit. I had to wear it because I was doing a funeral, but I'd much rather have had my bulky camouflage hunting coveralls on to keep me warm in the blustery wind. Since I didn't, I hugged my Bible to my chest and ran into the funeral home as quickly as my stiff legs would let me.

I wasn't really happy to be there, though when are you ever happy to be at a funeral? It was for an elderly lady who had been found dead in her little home. She died of natural causes, but as the Police Chaplain, I had still been called to meet the family when they arrived from a nearby town where they lived. As happened on several occasions, I was the only minister they knew, and they asked me, a virtual total stranger, to do the funeral service.

It's difficult to do a memorial service for someone you don't know, but it's even harder when you don't know a single person in the family. It always saddens me that there are people who do not know a minister of the gospel anywhere, not to mention one they could call "ours." It's hard for those of us whose lives are enveloped by church, brethren, and a spiritual extended family to understand how folks go through their entire lives without that kind of support system in place.

It got worse. After the music ended and it was my turn to speak, I was literally speechless for a minute or two as I faced the four people in attendance. All I could think of was "This lady had lived eight decades and only four people care that she has died!" It was all I could do not to rebuke the tiny assemblage of mourners for having such a poor turn-out. But, they were mourners, and hopefully the value of a person's life does not depend on the number of attendees at their funeral. I know that is true, but I kept thinking of the bald-headed detective on TV with a Tootsie Roll Pop™ in his mouth asking, "Who loves ya, baby?" It just seemed, at least for this poor deceased lady, that four was a pretty puny number.

It is on occasions like this that the truth of the statement, "Life is all about who you love and who loves you," really rings loudly. I've never officiated or even attended a funeral where the focus was on "things" that the deceased accumulated. I've never heard a financial report either. The emphasis is always on how much they were loved and how much they will be missed. The degrees, honors, and achievements pale to insignificance in the greater glow of human relationships. It would be nice if most of us could learn that long before there's a need for a eulogy.

It is an undeniable truth, we all love to be loved. Even if the relationship is not that deep, we all like to be liked. It's a natural part of our psychological and emotional make up. Our self-esteem desires it, and we will do almost anything to get it. We can be incredibly unselfish and sacrificial in our attempts to gain acceptance and recognition, and if that driving force is misdirected towards the wrong kind of people, we can become incredibly devious and wicked just to receive that same acceptance and recognition from them.

Sometimes the desire to be likable and lovable to others is so strong that we don't care if we are likable and lovable to God. The two are not necessarily mutually exclusive. It is possible to be loved by others and by God. In fact, a good steward of God's gifts, will not only try to please God but his or her fellow man. God's will must always come first, of course, but even He told us that the way to love Him was to love one another (1 John 4:7-21).

I've always been intrigued by the way those outside of the church viewed the church during those early days. At the end of Acts chapter 2, the church in Jerusalem was over three thousand strong. There was excitement in the air and activity everywhere. They were together a lot, and seeing to one another's needs. This didn't go unnoticed by others. The Bible says,

> And day by day continuing with one mind in the temple, and breaking bread from house to house, they were taking their meals together with gladness and sincerity of heart, praising God, and having favor with all the people. And the Lord was adding to their number day by day those who were being saved (Acts 2:46-47).

Clearly, both God and the people were pleased with what they saw. The people were impressed by their love for one another, their excitement about Jesus, and their care for those in need. They wanted to be part of something like that. So God blessed the early church with daily additions to His Body. Granted, those outside of the church didn't always view the church with such positive eyes, but it does teach us that favor with God and man is possible.

You've probably already jumped ahead and remembered that Jesus showed us the same thing. We've been looking at what was said about His growth, in Luke 2:52, and using it in this study of stewardship. Since He was a good steward of all He did, His growth in wisdom, stature, with God, and with man are all areas where we need to be good stewards too. We need to notice that He did grow "in favor with God and men," and it certainly wasn't a contradiction of purpose or the joining of things that were mutually exclusive.

What does it mean that He grew in favor with both God and man? It means that He was liked by both. We know that God was "well pleased" with Him, as He personally declared that at Jesus' baptism (Matt 3:17) and His transfiguration (Matt 17:5). We often miss the point that He was well liked by nearly everyone who ever met Him. The only individuals who didn't like Him were the religious leaders who felt threatened. The average people, especially the poor, the outcast, and the hurting, were attracted to Him like bees to honey. He was likable — not because he was attractive, domineering, or had some mystical aura about Him, but because He was genuine, caring, and unpretentious. He was God in the flesh and man is made in His image. Why wouldn't we like Him?

I believe with all my heart that the more we are like Jesus, the more people will like us. I'm talking about the real Jesus. Not some imagined "holier-than-thou" man-made image of Jesus as only a "temple cleaner" or a denouncer of Pharisees. The real Jesus was a people person. He loved everyone who would allow himself to be loved by Him, and He let that love show. He was forgiving, without endorsing sin; He was moved by compassion without being maudlin; He touched the untouchable without being condescending. The real Jesus was "real," and people liked Him — many loved Him.

On many occasions, it was the sheer number of people who liked Him that prevented the religious authorities from arresting Him and carrying out their plan to kill Him (see Matt 21:46). There is no denying the fact that many people were angered by His declaring Himself to be the Son of God, and others were incensed when He pointed out the inconsistencies in their spiritual lives. His own hometown seemed to have the most difficulty in accepting Him as the Messiah, but that may have been a matter of guilt on their part since they knew He knew them so well. Nevertheless, these rejections were few and expected. The multitudes were drawn to Him and sought His presence to the point of robbing Him of any private time.

We live to worship God. Stewardship is the expression of that worship as we are consistently obedient to God with every element of our lives. We have been emphasizing the total nature of our relationship with God and showing how these biblical concepts all reinforce that totality. Worship, obedience, glorifying, serving, and stewardship, are virtually synonyms for what God wants from us. All of these concepts are, and should be, expressed by our being Christlike. If we are Christlike, we will, like Jesus, grow in favor with God and man.

How, where, and when? Our obligation to Jesus and to our fellow man meet at the Cross. At the Cross we are confronted by our sinfulness and saved by His grace, but it's also at the Cross that we receive our commission to share it with others. Paul put the two together in 2 Corinthians 5:17-21 when he described every child of God as "a new creature" because of the Cross. This newness or forgiveness is part of the "riches of His grace, which He lavished upon us" (Eph 1:7-8). Paul reminds us that it all comes from God, "who reconciled us to Himself through Christ, and gave us the ministry of reconciliation . . . . Therefore, we are ambassadors for Christ, as though God were entreating through us; we beg you on behalf of Christ, be reconciled to God" (2 Cor 5:18,20).

We owe Him — because of the Cross! But, because of the Cross, we also owe the world Him! We owe it to Him and the world to be . . .

CROSS CARRIERS

I read an apocryphal story once about a monk who desperately wanted to be Christlike. He prayed and prayed and became so devoted to the task that he asked God to give him the marks of Jesus on his hands and feet. Rather than receiving the marks, he received a dream from God. In the dream he was shown a mark on Jesus' body that the world had forgotten about. It was the mark on His shoulder. The cuts, scrapes, and bruises came from the weight of the cross He carried through the streets of Jerusalem. The monk learned that before he could have the marks of Jesus on his hands and feet, he would first have to have the mark on his shoulder.[12]

Jesus' call for us to be cross carriers is probably one of the best known passages in the Gospels. He said,

> If any one wishes to come after Me, let him deny himself, and take up his cross, and follow Me. For whoever wishes to save his life shall lose it; but whoever loses his life for My sake shall find it. For what will a man be profited, if he gains the whole world, and forfeits his soul? Or what will a man give in exchange for his soul? (Matt 16:24-26).

This is a very powerful and convicting passage for all of us. What would you say the key word in this passage is? "Cross"? Maybe "deny" or "follow"? If you look closely, you will see that everything hinges on the little word "wishes." It is the key to the whole passage. If you "wish to" follow

Jesus, means if you "want, desire, or seek it." How badly do you want it? Jesus isn't looking for loafers looking for loaves. He isn't interested in having an entourage or a retinue of attendants. He didn't even need a group of bodyguards around Him, as Peter learned when he rebuked Him for saying that He'd be killed in Jerusalem. Peter essentially said that he wouldn't let it happen, and Jesus promptly told him to "Get behind Me, Satan! You are a stumbling block to Me; for you are not setting your mind on God's interests, but man's" (16:23). That was one of the reasons why Jesus went on to point out what real discipleship was all about.

Jesus is challenging every wannabe disciple with, "Do you know what you want? If you really want to follow me, it's going to cost you plenty! You have to deny your desires, your plans, and your very life. Then you must freely pick up a cross, which is My yoke with all the trials that come with it, and walk in My footsteps. I will lead you, be with you, comfort you, and support you, and if you lose your life in the process, I'll personally give you a perfect eternal replacement. So — do you still want to be My disciple?"

To be a good steward of our cross, we can't carry any baggage along with it. It's the cross and the cross only. Other baggage like guilt, selfishness, and pride, must be dumped and left behind. That's part of denying self. We can't carry His cross in one hand and personal baggage in the other. His cross is a two-handed, shoulder-cutting burden that takes our total focus and all our strength. Only then does He help us shoulder it so that His load becomes light.

We can't hang our idols on it like it was some kind of Christmas tree. All idols must be forsaken and forgotten. As Paul did, we must count all things as refuse or garbage in order that we might gain Christ, ". . . that I may know Him, and the power of His resurrection and the fellowship of His sufferings, being conformed to His death; in order that I may attain to the resurrection from the dead" (Phil 3:10-11).

As we grow in favor with God and men, men need to see that we are cross carriers. They not only need to see it, they need to hear it. We owe it to God and the world to be . . .

CROSS BOASTERS

What do you brag about? If we were talking face to face, you'd probably be offended and say, "I don't brag about anything. I try to be a very humble person." The truth is we all brag about something occasionally. It's human nature to brag. There's a competitive gene in all of us that drives us to want to win, be first, or the best whenever we can. It's like the jingle from an old dog food commercial. Remember this? "My dog's bigger then your dog. My dog's bigger than yours. My dog's bigger 'cause he eats KenL Ration™. My dog's bigger than yours." If you remember hearing it on TV you just dated yourself.

We brag about what's important to us. It may be our athletic ability, our intellect, our accomplishments, or our successes. People brag about their school, their families, their favorite teams, and their country. Some even brag about their failures, mistakes, and rejections, especially when they are the worst. The young brag about their future while the elderly brag about their past. The middle-aged brag about not being either one. The young have trophies to show, and the older generation has pictures of grandchildren to show. Members regularly brag about their church, preachers brag about their preaching, and elders brag about their lack of control. I've even heard people brag about how humble they are, which means if they were, they aren't anymore.

Bragging is not always wrong. If it's prideful and haughty then it always is, but sometimes it comes from a godly heart. If it wells up from a thankful heart, it may just be rejoicing. If I said, "It's great to be a child of God!" and it came from gratefulness and joy in Christ, it wouldn't be bragging in a bad sense — though it's certainly bragging. With the right kind of spirit behind it, bragging may just be a declaration of fact. The real question is, whom are we exalting? If we are exalting God and Jesus, as we do in many of our praise songs, then it's a confession not conceit.

Paul said it beautifully in Galatians 6:14: "But may it never be that I should boast, except in the cross of our Lord Jesus Christ, through which the world has been crucified to me, and I to the world."

Let me repeat it. We brag about what is important to us. Paul said he only wanted to brag about one thing in his life — the Cross of Christ. Why? Because it was the most important thing in his life. Everything else was trivial!

The context of this declaration by Paul is self-righteousness. Many were proud of their Hebrew heritage and boasted in their loyalty to the Law. We can't imagine it in our culture today, but back then they bragged about being circumcised. It was a fleshly sign of righteousness that ignored grace and liberty in Christ. Paul said that we need to boast in what Jesus has done, not what we have done.

Do you ever do more bragging about your accomplishments than you do about what Jesus did? We said at the beginning of this chapter that we all like to be liked by people. It's not wrong to want that, but it is wrong to promote yourself to the exclusion of promoting Jesus. It takes time to build relationships, to develop a sense of trust and confidence in others, but sooner or later we need to stop selling ourselves and start bragging about Jesus.

He is more important than our family, our country, our school, our jobs, and even our congregation. What He did for us on the cross is more than what anyone who ever lived ever even dreamed of doing for us. He loved us and died for us while we were helpless, ungodly, sinners, and enemies (Rom 5:6-10). He washed us in His blood, taking away all our sin, and He continues to wash us as we walk in His light (1 John 1:7).

You and I have never done anything for anyone, even ourselves, that matches what Jesus did for us. Because of that, our accomplishments and achievements become blessings, and our experiences, whether good or bad, become gifts from God. Whatever happens, whether we live or whether we die, we are the Lord's (Rom 14:8). He will make things work together for our good (Rom 8:28), and He will personally protect us from condemnation (Rom 8:1).

In view of what He has done for us, there is really nothing else worth boasting about. Paul was making that same argument to those who would boast in the Law. He said, "I died to the Law, that I might live to God." Then he described what it means to live to God.

> I have been crucified with Christ; and it is no longer I who live, but Christ lives in me; and the *life* which I now live in the flesh I live by faith in the Son of God, who loved me, and delivered Himself up for me (Gal. 2:19-20).

What else is there to boast about after you have been crucified with Christ? Even in hardship and suffering, we boast about how God will use it to teach us and prepare us for greater service in His Kingdom. Once Paul realized that God did His greatest work in our lives during times of weakness, he declared, "Most gladly, therefore, I will rather boast about my weaknesses, that the power of Christ may dwell in me" (2 Cor 12:9). When a "thorn in the flesh" or some kind of serious problem becomes an opportunity for us to boast about the Cross of Jesus Christ, then we are getting a handle on what it means to be a good steward of our cross.

As we grow in favor with God and men, men need to see that we are cross boasters. They also need to see that we are . . .

CROSS LIFTERS

You're probably asking yourself, "What's the difference between being a cross boaster and a cross lifter?" The answer is, little or nothing. I choose little. I want to emphasize, one more time, how important it is to display Jesus in our lives. Being a cross carrier is our personal decision to live for Him. A cross boaster shares the message of the Cross because it is the most important thing there is to talk about. A cross lifter holds up Jesus by the way he lives. He sets the example for others. He holds up nothing that others can rally around except the Cross of Jesus Christ.

We've examined the need for consistency in every point we've made. I want to, as they say, "Turn the heat up a little bit." Cross lifting is obvious Christianity. It's visible, commendable, and imitable. It's lifting a cross up through dedicated and consistent living that is not seeking recognition for self, but recognition for Jesus.

I am a Civil War history buff. Its official name, according to the Congressional Record is "The War of the Rebellion." Many in the South still call it "The War of Northern Aggression." Whether your historical leanings are for the North or the South, we all must agree that it was a horrendous tragedy that took more American lives than all of the other American wars combined. The devastation and death were so terrible because of the combination of modern weapons used in an old European style of warfare. They literally just lined up facing each other and blazed away with powerful and fairly accurate guns.

This type of warfare required incredible courage on the part of all the participants. I can't imagine what kind of courage it took to charge an entrenched position with thousands of rifles and cannons being fired at you. The most courageous of all were the color bearers – the men who held their flags high for everyone else to rally around. Not only were they obvious targets, but they couldn't fire their guns and wave the flag at the same time. Add to that the high motivation that the other side had to try to capture an opponent's flag, and the poor color bearer was a sitting duck.

Yet in spite of that risk, there was never a shortage of people willing to carry the flag in battle. We have incredible documentation for every battle of the war. There were battles where dozens were killed or wounded carrying the same flag. One would be shot and someone else would pick it up and continue the charge. Amazing courage, but amazing carnage. All for a cause they were willing to die for.

We don't have a flag to wave, but we do have a Cross to lift up. We lift it up when we help others see in us the Jesus who died for their sins. We make a terrible mistake when we lift ourselves up to be seen by men. Even if it is done in the name of Jesus, if the focus is on us and not Him, it is hypocrisy and pride. We must be like John the Baptist when he said that he would necessarily decrease, but the Lord must increase.

The Jewish leaders and the Roman soldiers who did the deed made a big mistake when they crucified Jesus. Yes, it was part of God's plan for redeeming man, but that's not what they thought they were doing. They thought that they were putting an end to all the speculation and controversy over whether or not this Jewish carpenter was the Messiah. It backfired on them. Jesus had said, "And I, if I be lifted up from the earth, will draw all men to Myself" (John 12:32). They made a big mistake when they lifted Him up on that cross. It wasn't the end but the beginning. It did settle once and for all the validity of His Messiahship, but not the way they thought it would.

The church makes a big mistake when it lifts up the Body without the Head. Jesus, and His Cross, must be the focal point of everything the church does. A program or ministry that is lifted up in place of the Cross is nothing more than a work of man. An assembly of the saints that

doesn't lift up the Cross of Jesus is at best religious ritualism and at worst a social club.

Jesus said that loving one another is what identifies us as
His disciples to the world (John 13:35). When we love one
another we are lifting up His Cross for the world to see.
Sadly enough, many are so interested in lifting up their
preferences and opinions, and seeking to get what they
want out of the assembly time, that all the world sees is
bickering and complaining, not people lifting up crosses.
The Cross of Jesus is put on the back burner while the selfish war between the progressives and the traditionalists
dominates the menu.

The Cross is lifted up when brethren assemble together
to "stimulate one another to love and good deeds," and to
encourage one another (Heb 10:24-25). The Cross is lifted
up when we look for ways to build others up, bear one
another's burdens, and seek to "Let all things be done for
edification" (1 Cor 14:26). In the New Testament assembly,
encouragement and edification were always things Christians
did for others, not what they went expecting to have
happen to themselves.

The Cross is never lifted up by church politics, petty
quarreling, and selfish agendas. We have only one agenda,
and that is to lift up the Cross of Jesus in everything we do
individually and as a congregation.

The words of the following poem speak to the importance of our being Cross-oriented in all we do. The anony-
mous poet says,

> I counted dollars while God counted crosses.
> I counted gains while He counted losses!
> I counted my worth by the things gained in store.
> But He sized me up by the scars that I bore.
> I coveted honors and sought for degrees;
> He wept as He counted the hours on my knees.
> And I never knew 'til one day at the grave,
> How vain are these things that we spend life to save![13]

Several years ago there was a popular action movie that simply took the audience from one cliffhanger to another. The title was "The Jewel of the Nile." Through most of the movie, the handsome hero thought he was on a treasure hunt for a valuable jewel that would make him unbelievably rich when he found it. To his surprise, the Jewel of the Nile turned out to be a little holy man, who was indeed very valuable to his fellow countrymen. The Jewel of the Nile wasn't a precious stone, but a precious person.

What is the Cross of Christ? What is it that we lift up for all men to see? The Cross of Christ is not a wooden beam, but a heart full of Jesus. It isn't a trophy to be displayed, but a burden of gratefulness that humbles us. It's not a big stick to beat others into submission, but a gentle spirit that is "moved with compassion" just like the One who was nailed to it. It is a life "hidden in Christ" but not hiding Christ.

You denied self, took up your cross, and followed Him. Are you a good steward of that cross? Where is it? Does it need to be dusted off and picked back up? There are people who need to see it. Jesus needs to see it!

I am reminded of the words in that old classic song:

Must Jesus bear the cross alone, and all the world go free?
No, there's a cross for everyone, and there's a cross for me!

DISCUSSION QUESTIONS

1. Is it true that life is all about those you love and who loves you? Why?

2. Why do you think the first converts to Christianity were attracted to the church? (See Acts 2:46-47.)

3. During Jesus' earthly ministry, who liked Him and didn't like Him? Why?

4. Why do we not feel a sense of obligation to share the gospel with the lost?

5. What kind of "extra baggage" do we sometimes carry around instead of the Cross of Christ?

CHAPTER TEN
Stewards of His Church

The little boy came into the auditorium after his Bible class on Sunday morning. The class that week had been on the first few chapters of Genesis. As his mother came up to him, she noticed the worried look on his face as he held his hand to his side. She asked, "What's the matter Billy?" After rubbing his side a little, he answered, "I don't know Mom, but I think I'm having a wife." He'd obviously missed the point of the Genesis story.

It was Question and Answer time for the disciples as they traveled down the road with Jesus. They happened to pass by a man who had been born blind and therefore was forced to live in darkness and beg for handouts his whole life. They didn't see an opportunity to serve but rather an opportunity to ask a theological question. They wondered whose sin had caused the man to be blind. Was it his or his parents' sins? To them, blindness was obviously a curse or punishment for sin, so who was the guilty party?

Jesus emphatically pointed out that it had nothing to do with sin, and everything to do with an opportunity to glorify God. Jesus healed him. A man who had always been blind and had always begged for money from all the people in town was now healed, and it didn't go unnoticed. It caused such a stir that the Pharisees decided to sit in judgment on the act. They didn't care that a man who'd spent his life blind was given his sight. They didn't care that God's power had been displayed in a mighty way. All they cared about was that Jesus healed somebody on the Sabbath. This incredible proof of His Sonship was seen by them as proof that He wasn't from God. They said, "This man is not from God, because He does not keep the Sabbath" (John 9:1-16). Of course, He did keep the Sabbath, just not their traditions about the Sabbath. Talk about missing the point! They couldn't see the forest of compassion for the trees of their tradition.

"I just don't get anything out of it," cries Charlie the Church-Goer. "The singing just doesn't grab me. The songs are too slow, too old, and too irrelevant. There's no spirit — no enthusiasm — no energy. It's the same old schedule, the same old rituals, and the same old sermons. It just doesn't push my buttons any more. If something doesn't change pretty soon, I'm going to have to look for a new church to attend. One that will make me feel good about going to church and not make me feel like I'm wasting my time."

"I just don't get anything out of it," moans Tommy Tradition. "The singing sounds like a Rock Concert. People are clapping their hands like it was some kind of hoedown, and there's no reverence or respect for the presence of God and the formal worship service. All they want to do is change everything. There's no security, dependability, and predictability anymore. I miss the old ways. The way we used to do worship. It was good enough for us when we were young, and it's good enough for us today. I'm just so uncomfortable with all this new stuff — this anti-tradition stuff, that I'm going to have to find another church that is loyal to the 'Old Paths.'"

Like the little boy, who was "having a wife," and like the Pharisees in John 9, both Charlie and Tommy have missed the point. They have missed the point of what church is all about.

If we could get honest answers, it would be informative to know what the average member thinks the purpose of the church is. I mention getting honest answers because in a church setting people are always going to give the expected scriptural answer. "Why, the purpose of the church is to take the gospel to the lost," some would surely say. Others would say, "Well, the church exists to carry out the will of God on earth." There would be an endless list of good and generic answers. But what does your heart really say the purpose of the church is?

Some really honest answers would be that the purpose of the church is:

✦ to meet twice on Sunday and once on Wednesday.

✦ to provide a place for Christians to worship God.

✦ to provide for me a sense of continuity and security in my life. I need to know that it won't change.

✦ to make me feel good when I go to church.

✦ to provide excitement and enthusiasm that lifts me up.

✦ to teach me the Word of God.

✦ to provide me with an opportunity to pray.

✦ to train my children in the way they should go.

✦ to make me feel like I belong.

✦ to meet all my needs.

✦ to make sure that all members are doctrinally correct.

✦ to sit in judgment on every member and determine whether their past sins are forgiven or not.

✦ to make sure that I have an opportunity to serve in some way.

✦ to expect nothing more from me than attendance and a check.

✦ to provide me with nothing but positive experiences.

✦ to make sure that my money is not misspent.

The possibilities could fill up the rest of this book. Hopefully you are seeing the point that many Christians miss the point. These things are not the purpose of the church. While some of the above may be things a congregation might choose to do, most of them are selfish, prideful, and worldly views of what the church is all about. If it were possible to be truly honest, many would have to say, "The church exists to please me."

Members want to have their needs met rather than try to meet the needs of others. We "go to church" to "get, receive, take, and experience" not to give, share, and serve others. The church is not the Body of Christ but an institution to be protected and preserved. We say it is not a building or a place, but that is so ingrained in our psyche that we can't ignore it. Church is what we *are* not where we *go*. We are the Lord's church whether we are alone or together. He added us to His church (Acts 2:41), and He doesn't remove us when we're not together. We are always His church. The church is not organizations, programs, and ministries. It's people who belong to Jesus! Church is not something that happens one or two hours on Sunday. It's people who belong to Jesus wherever they are and whatever time it is.

Church isn't a system of doctrines, a body of beliefs, or an exclusive society. It isn't an institution with traditions, by-laws, and rituals. It isn't real estate, or facilities, or a social program. It isn't determined by deeds, directories, or databases. It's a spiritual body, an eternal family, and the membership is recorded in heaven.

A brief survey of Paul's letter to the Ephesians gives us a clear definition of what the purpose of the church is. First it must be headed by Jesus and by Him alone.

And He put all things in subjection under His feet, and gave Him as head over all things to the church, which is His body, the fullness of Him who fills all in all (Eph 1:22-23).

He is not only the head, but the church is His body, in total submission to Him. That is only appropriate since . . .

> God, being rich in mercy, because of His great love with which He loved us, even when we were dead in our transgressions, made us alive together with Christ (by grace you have been saved), and raised us up with Him, and seated us with Him in the heavenly *places*, in Christ Jesus (2:4-6).

Because of this great love and this great gift of grace, we . . .

> . . . are fellow-citizens with the saints, and are of God's household, having been built upon the foundation of the apostles and prophets, Christ Jesus Himself being the corner *stone*, in whom the whole building, being fitted together is growing into a holy temple in the Lord; in whom you also are being built together into a dwelling of God in the Spirit (vv. 19-22).

The church is a spiritual building, built on Jesus, and growing into a "holy temple" and a "dwelling" place of God and the Spirit. Did you notice the emphasis on "together"? We are "fitted" and "built" together" by God. So we are a church individually, and we are a church collectively, because it is all spiritual construction, not physical construction. Wherever Jesus lives, it's His church, and His church must do His will.

Paul was an apostle and a missionary to the Gentile world. He was also part of the church. His description of his purpose is also a description of the church's purpose. He said that he was called to share . . .

> . . . the unfathomable riches of Christ, and to bring to light what is the administration of the mystery which for ages has been hidden in God, who created all things; in order that the manifold wisdom of God might now be made known through the church to the rulers and the authori-

ties in the heavenly *places. This was* in accordance with the eternal purpose which He carried out in Christ Jesus our Lord (3:8-11).

It is through the church that God's plan for redeeming man is to be shared to a world in darkness. God planned it that way before creation. The church was to be His vehicle to take His message about His love and grace to everyone.

This doesn't mean that the church has only one ministry — outreach. We must meet together and organize to a certain degree to bring about "the equipping of the saints for the work of service, to the building up of the body of Christ; until we all attain to the unity of the faith, and of the knowledge of the Son of God, to a mature man, to the measure of the stature which belongs to the fullness of Christ" (4:12-13). After all, Jesus said that the world would recognize us as belonging to Him because of the special love we have for one another (John 13:35).

The church is in the growing, equipping, and loving-one-another business — but that is to help it carry out its purpose as a bringer of light to a world of darkness. We have institutionalized the equipping and ignored the sharing. It is not an either/or proposition but a both/and proposition. We must equip so that "the proper working of each individual part causes the growth of the body for the building up of itself in love"(4:16). That growth is in both spiritual maturity in members and the "adding to [our] number day by day those who [are] being saved" (Acts 2:47).

The purpose of the church is to bring about a spiritual intimacy and love among brethren that authenticates our message about the love of God to the lost. Both individually and collectively we must be good stewards of that purpose. Are we?

I have already mentioned that the church seems to be equipping while not sharing, but are we really equipping if it doesn't lead to sharing? If we are not good stewards of the sharing part of our purpose, is that because we aren't good stewards of the "spiritual intimacy and love among brethren" part? Could this be why so many have a distorted, selfish, and unbiblical perspective on the purpose of the church?

STEWARDS OF TOGETHERNESS

Whether you've studied history books or simply read James Michener's *Texas*, you know that Texas has a very rich, colorful, and exciting history. While much of it has been glorified and several aspects covered by the mantle of Manifest Destiny (American Indians, Mexican-Americans, and Afro-Americans have different interpretations than most Texas historians), it is an inspiring story of struggle, unity, and victory. In fact, one of Michener's major themes in his epic account of Texas was unity in adversity. The early Texans were drawn together because of a common enemy. Originally, it was Indians, then later it was the Mexican Army, and after becoming a State it was the Indians again. (In the twentieth century the enemy has been the Washington Redskins).

Unity is nearly always a beautiful thing to behold. It's commendable and flattering to any group that can achieve it. Maybe that is one of the reasons why God wants the Body of Christ to be united. It glorifies God since it is obedience to Him, but it also glorifies God because of the positive message it sends to the world.

Unity in Christ is or should be like no other unity. Yes, like the early Texans, there is a common enemy, but more importantly we have a common Lord. Our oneness in Christ should transcend race, economics, education, gender, class, age, culture, and anything else that divides, labels, or by worldly standards alienates people. The blood of Jesus washed away our sins and sets us on the road to removing prejudice, pride, and feelings of superiority from our lives.

The first Christians in the first congregation seemed to understand this uncommon unity that Jesus called for. By the end of Acts chapter four, there are several thousand Christians in Jerusalem with more being added every day. We've looked at the excitement felt by the first three thousand converts when we examined Acts 2, but the description of the early church in chapter four is even more encouraging.

There is a series of events leading up to the passage I want to discuss that all began with an interruption of Peter and John's plan to pray. At the beginning of Acts chapter three, they heal a lame man who was sitting at one of the gates of the temple. This attracted a crowd, to whom Peter preached the gospel. Many of the crowd believed their message, and this greatly disturbed the priests and the Sadducees. Peter and John were arrested and put in jail. This gave them a chance to witness before the rulers, elders, scribes, and priests. They boldly proclaimed Jesus as the Messiah. The council threatened them and warned them to stop preaching Jesus, but Peter and John simply told them that they had to obey God not man. They were threatened again, but released unharmed. This caused all the Christians in Jerusalem to rejoice and glorify God and speak the message of Jesus with even more boldness (Acts 4:31).

We thus find ourselves at the closing verses of chapter four, where the Holy Spirit guided Luke to give a beautiful summation of what the church in Jerusalem was doing.

> And the congregation of those who believed were of one heart and soul; and not one *of them* claimed that anything belonging to him was his own; but all things were common property to them (v. 32).

Wouldn't you love for that to be said about your congregation? I hear of congregations today that are described as "progressive," "traditional," "on the cutting edge," and even "great givers," but there is nothing better that could be said about a group of believers than that they are "of one heart and soul." Being of "one heart" speaks to their emotional attachment. They loved each other. When people are of one heart, they know each other well enough to deeply care about each other. A once-a-week handshake with a "hi" and "bye" in the foyer is not an emotional attachment. They had a depth in their relationship that allowed them to know about each other's needs.

The "one soul" part of the description speaks to the spiritual level of their relationship, which only added depth and significance to their emotional attachment. They were together! They shared experiences, prayed, praised, and pondered their walk with God. Brethren who are of one heart and soul are not passing acquaintances.

This is why they did not think of their "stuff" as being possessions they owned. This is not, as some have called it, pure communism or utopianism, it's stewardship. When you really understand that you've gone from being lost to being found, from being in darkness to being in light, and from being dead to being truly alive — who cares about stuff! They had an emotional and spiritual attachment that meant that everything they owned was a gift to be shared not a treasure to be possessed. In Christ we go from ownership to stewardship!

In a land of plenty and affluence this may be one of the toughest lessons we can learn. We are into accumulation not generosity, possession not compassion, and hoarding rather than hope. It's more important to us to have goods than to do good. We want brethren to be impressed with our standard of living rather than being impressed with our standard of giving. We require a respectful distance between brethren, which means once the final "Amen" is heard on Sunday morning, "respectfully keep your distance."

Our cultural philosophy has become our theology. The world invented it, and we promote it. It's a "what's mine is mine and what's yours is yours" attitude where stewardship isn't even part of the formula. We've fostered an attitude that says, "Church is a middle-class club, and if you have any physical needs, don't let anyone in the church know about it." If someone does need help and they ask, they are treated and thought of as slackers, inept, and maybe even crooked or at least suspicious.

We love to say that we are just like the New Testament Christians, but we've seen very few Christians today who think of what they have not as their own, but things to be used to help others. That's called selective biblical application. "It was just a cultural thing," someone declares, "and not applicable today." That is always a convenient out, and a good way to protect our stuff.

Somehow, some way, we need to restore the emotional and spiritual closeness of the New Testament church. Their love, compassion, and unselfishness towards one another is the true essence of stewardship. Their relationship was based on caring and sharing, not three songs, a prayer, and a check in the plate.

> For there was not a needy person among them, for all who were owners of land or houses would sell them and bring the proceeds of the sales, and lay them at the apostles feet; and they would be distributed to each, as any had need (vv. 34-35).

Stewardship within a congregation is only possible and meaningful if there is intimacy in the congregation. If there is no intimacy, there is little or no stewardship. To reject or not foster intimacy in your congregation is to reject stewardship. We can't respond to needs that we don't know about, and we'd just as soon not know.

In this megachurch in Jerusalem, there wasn't a single person in need who didn't have that need taken care of by brethren. Is that true for your congregation? Is there any needy person in your church family? At best you have to answer, "I hope not." The real answer is "I don't know."

Is that your fault for not knowing, or their fault for not telling you? God wants us to be together, to help each other with our burdens, to build each other up, and to keep each other focused on Jesus and His return. He wants us to have *koinonia*, which is a deep fellowship and communion in Christ. Why is it that "the folks at church" are the last people in the world you'd want to know that you were having a problem or had some special need? Why is it that brethren with needs just disappear rather than share their need with their congregation? Something is very different from what it was in the New Testament church.

Could it be that our formalism, our sanctuary mind-set about worship, and our institutionalizing of church have robbed us of genuine one-another "heart and soul" intimacy? Where did we get the idea that Christians are supposed to be perfect, without any problems? We confirm that by faithful attendance, wearing our church uniform, and having a reverential expression. We spout off orthodoxy, do our "five acts," shake hands with other perfect people, and get mad if someone suggests changing our traditional way of doing things. If we move or change churches, it's two months before anyone notices, and the ripple effect is nonexistent.

You might be thinking, "Well, that's an awfully harsh judgment on the church." I understand that, but in your heart, because you've been a student of the Word, you know that it's true. I'm not interested in church-bashing or tradition-bashing. Contrary to what some who've read my other books think, I do not have a chip on my shoulder nor do I hold a grudge towards the church over some mistreatment in the past. I do, however, have a love for Jesus, His church, and His will. I was trained by godly men and women to respect His Word, and to have a passion to be "simply and only a New Testament Christian." What I see in the New Testament church of the Bible is not what I see in the church of today.

Sure, there are brethren who are compassionate, sensitive, unselfish, and servant oriented. There are folks in every congregation who are wonderful examples of what it means to be a good steward, but they are the minority. We've heard all our lives about the eighty and twenty rule. Eighty percent of the work of the church is done by twenty percent of the members. Often it's less than that. A huge chunk of the membership of every church is people who want absolutely no other responsibility than to attend "worship" one hour on Sunday morning. You have to chase them down just to shake their hands before they rush out of the building — assuming they wait for the final "Amen."

Where's the "one heart and soul" intimacy? Where's the "not a needy person among them" sharing that the New Testament church had? We all have folks in our congregations who would request food stamps from the government before they'd ask anyone in the church for help. Not that there's anything wrong with food stamps, but if God didn't want the world to see one brother taking another brother to court (1 Cor 6:1-11), how much more would He not want the world to see us neglect one of our own who was in need? Paul told us "So then, while we have opportunity, let us do good to all men, and especially to those who are of the household of the faith" (Gal 6:10).

Are we looking for opportunities to do good? Are we especially looking for those opportunities within the "household of the faith?" What we have is reverse "Hide and Seek!" Those of a family who are in need are hiding, the rest of us aren't seeking, and those hiding want to keep it that way. Thus we all contribute to poor stewardship of our togetherness. Our church structure fosters it, and our personal pride insists on it.

These words of Paul need some serious contemplation:

Let love be without hypocrisy. Abhor what is evil; cling to what is good. Be devoted to one another in brotherly love; give preference to one another in honor; not lagging

174

behind in diligence, fervent in spirit, serving the Lord; rejoicing in hope, persevering in tribulation, devoted to prayer, contributing to the needs of the saints, practicing hospitality (Rom 12:9-13).

STEWARDS OF WITNESSING

We will become good stewards of His church when we realize that we have brethren to love and a world to witness to. Are they connected to each other? Absolutely! Witnessing is simply having a story to tell, just like a witness in a trial. Our story is that Jesus saved us and made a difference in our lives. Being "one heart and soul" with His family is part of that difference. When we don't experience that devotion and intimacy, that deep caring and meeting of needs, then our witness will be weak.

Remember what the pivotal proof was in Peter's first sermons? On the day of Pentecost, when he preached the first gospel sermon, he told them that Jesus was the Messiah. They, however, had crucified Him and placed His body in a tomb. Then he declared, "This Jesus God raised up again, to which we are all witnesses" (Acts 2:32). He wasn't just proclaiming that Jesus rose from the dead. He said, "I saw Him! I was an eyewitness!"

He preached the same thing to the next crowd. It was after the healing of the lame man in Acts 3. He told them that God raised Jesus from the dead "*a fact* to which we are witnesses" (v. 15). In the first instance, three thousand became Christians. In the second instance, the number jumped to five thousand. One would have to say that it was a powerful witness.

In the midst of describing the closeness and unselfishness of the early church, who were of "one heart and soul" and met every need of every member, a similar reference is made.

And with great power the apostles were giving witness to
the resurrection of the Lord Jesus, and abundant grace was
upon them all (Acts 4:33).

Remember, this is in the middle of describing the incredible intimacy and spirit of sharing that the church in
Jerusalem had. Is the "great power" that the apostles had a
description of the Holy Spirit empowering them? Is it talking about their signs and miracles? Or could it be merely
talking about their enthusiasm and boldness that came
from seeing their new converts display such tenderness
and care for each other? Was it the excitement of a new
life of sharing and unity like they'd never experienced
before? If so, then it directly impacted their "witness."

When you see the power of a resurrected Christ change
lives, it's a story that begs to be told. It reinforces the fact
of that resurrection. It makes us "eyewitnesses" by faith,
just as surely as Peter was physically an eyewitness. The
resurrection of Jesus was the key doctrinal theme of all
early New Testament preaching. They didn't argue Scripture
or interpretation of texts. If Jesus was raised from the dead,
He clearly was the Son of God and obedience to Him was
the only logical next step. If He wasn't raised . . . well . . .
everything else is a waste of breath.

Have we lost our witness? Have we become so focused
on doctrinal minutia that we've forgotten the message that
Jesus died for our sins and God raised Him from the dead,
confirming that salvation is available to all who call on His
name? We are witnesses! His resurrection is a fact, and we
have seen its power in our lives and in the lives of brethren.
That's our story! It's not "personal work" or a deep theological discussion, but our telling others, "I've seen it!"

We can't proclaim to others that we have a living Lord
when we have a dead church. It destroys our witness. That
is not an excuse, it is a fact. There is always a handful of
brethren who are able to be motivated to witness regardless of what goes on at their congregation. It was God's

intent that our church family inspire us and help us grow to the point that we would witness about Jesus and want others to be part of our spiritual family.

Notice one final point from this wonderful and challenging passage about that first congregation in Jerusalem. Because of their great love for one another and the resulting witnessing that it caused, "abundant grace was upon them all." What does that mean? Did they have more grace at that point in their spiritual growth than when they first became Christians? Did they receive more grace than we do today? Is grace something that is given in degrees?

In his classic commentary on Acts, J.W. McGarvey did not believe that this "abundant grace" that was upon them was "the grace of God, which had been upon them uniformly from the beginning." He believed that it was describing the favor they had in the eyes of the community because of their great unity and sacrificial giving for one another.[14] I agree and would add that this "abundant grace" was also a description of the spirit that permeated their togetherness. Grace, at its fundamental essence, is giving even when the gift is not deserved. The loving, unselfish, and compassionate giving of this early church could not have been as complete as it was if there hadn't been an absence of pride, judging, and partiality. Grace was given to us by God to be given by us to others. It's the ultimate definition of stewardship.

When we achieve the kind of togetherness they had and find ourselves witnessing about what Jesus did and is doing in our church family, we will find out firsthand what it means to have "abundant grace" upon us.

DISCUSSION QUESTIONS

1. What does your heart tell you about the purpose of the church?

2. Why do we expect the worship assembly to "meet our needs?" Where did that come from?

3. Are we good stewards of our responsibilities to convince the world that His disciples love one another?

4. Could your congregation be described as being "of one heart and soul?" (Acts 4:32) Why or why not?

5. It was said of the early church, "there was not a needy person among them" because they took care of one another (Acts 4:34). Is that true of the church today? Why or why not?

6. If you started attending another congregation's assembly, how long would it take before anyone missed you? Why is that?

CHAPTER ELEVEN
Stewards of His Assembly

While driving home after the Sunday morning assembly, the wife who had been deep in thought finally asked, "Did you see that hat Mrs. Jones wore to church?" Her husband quickly answered, "Nope." "Well," she continued, "did you see the new dress Mrs. Smith had on?" Again her husband grunted, "Nope." With amazement on her face she said, "Well a lot of good it does you to go to church!"

As humorous as that may sound, I feel quite confident that a conversation like that, or something similar, has taken place many times. For several of my teenage years, "going to church" meant getting your best clothes on in order to impress the girls. Since I was attending a small, very conservative Christian boarding school, sitting with a girl during "worship" was as close to a date as we were likely to get. And since we were required to "dress up for church," we took full advantage of the opportunity to look our best. (Actually, in the sixties we wanted to look "groovy" not good.)

Our Sunday morning assemblies are steeped in nineteen centuries of tradition. Many of these traditions are so entrenched that members guard them with greater fervor than they do the Truth. Through the centuries the Christian assembly has gone from being a support system for togetherness and spiritual growth to being the focus of our religious life. It is the preeminent spiritual activity of our life. Attendance is the single most important element that defines faithfulness. Our group identity is not found in an obvious love for one another as Jesus wanted it, but in having all the correct "acts of worship" every time we meet.

The Christian assembly evolved from a simple meeting, a time of togetherness, and an opportunity for *koinonia* (deep spiritual fellowship), to a formal, reverential, and ritualistic event that every adherent is bound by law to attend. We developed facilities, furniture, and formal attire to fit the occasion, as man has defined it, and we have solemnized the event by building a rich tradition of meditation, with no interaction but with predictable structure. To bolster its importance, we have called the place "church" and the activity "worship," even though it is a very unbiblical use of both terms. Since we are already calling the Christian assembly something that the Bible doesn't call it, why not call it "a fashion show?"

In my two previous books, *Spilt Grape Juice* and *Unbroken Bread,* I dealt with these things in detail. At this point in this study, I just want to remind us all that the Christian assembly is not the center or focus of our spiritual lives. Our *lives* are worship to God. He is praised by our obedience to Him. He wants Christians to be together to build each other up and to encourage each other to be Christlike (Eph 4:11-16; Heb 10:21-25). When we do that, in obedience to God, it is worship, but no more than any other act of obedience would be. Stewardship is having a heart that wants to glorify God with everything He has given us. Stewardship is our life expressing worship to God.

While the assembly is not "THE worship," it is something He wants us to do. It is one of the gifts He has given us to help us "grow in the grace and knowledge of our Lord and Savior Jesus Christ." Since it is a gift from God, it must glorify Him. We must be good stewards of our assembly. While that must begin by having a biblical perspective on the purpose of the assembly, that is covered in the two books mentioned above. In our present study I want us to think about what we can do to be good stewards of our assembly. How can we make the most out of what we do when we are together? We will have one precondition to this discussion. How can we, as individuals, make the most out of our assembly *regardless of what everyone else does?!*

WHO OWES WHOM?

What does the church owe you? Forget the "appropriate answer" and don't allow yourself to sound self-righteous, just try to be honest. You do have expectations of what your congregation ought to do for you. What are they? Do they owe you inclusion, making sure that you are part of whatever goes on? Do they owe you an opportunity for input on every decision whether it's to change or not to change? Do they owe you support, encouragement, love, discipline, shepherding, opportunities, visits, and covered dish dinners when you're sick or bereaved? Do they owe you a reserved pew, a leadership position, a choice of Bible classes, a centrally heated and air-conditioned building, an appropriate assembly time, an evening assembly, and a midweek Bible class? Do they owe you an explanation for where your contributions are spent? Do they owe you comfort, security, predictability, and protection from change? Do they owe you excitement, entertainment, enthusiasm, a challenge, and the guarantee of constant change?

181

Notice that I emphasized "they" in reference to the church. The church is the Body of Christ and is made up of all those whom God has placed in it (Acts 2:41,47). It's people — people of God. It's not a building, an institution, or a corporation. Each congregation is a smaller part of the much larger Body. While we might organize to be efficient or for expediency, the local church is not an organization — it's a living, breathing, growing part of the Body of Christ. As previously discussed, its purpose is to facilitate Christian togetherness and witnessing. It's a support system not a structure or idol to be maintained or worshiped and praised in place of a personal walk with God. It is a tool to help carry out the will of God. Too many Christians are worshiping the tool and not the Tool Maker.

What does your local congregation owe you? It owes you what all churches owe their individual members, opportunities to be with other Christians and opportunities to grow. Everything else is either an expedient support of these two elements or it's fluff and tradition.

It may or may not provide spiritual leadership, nice facilities, and magnificent programs. Those are blessings and even luxuries, not requirements. It doesn't change our individual accountability to God and responsibility to our brethren. God provided apostles, prophets, evangelists, pastors, and teachers "for the equipping of the saints for the work of service, to the building up of the body of Christ" (Eph 4:11-12). After the first century, there weren't any more apostles and prophets. Many churches don't have pastors or evangelists, yet they manage to equip one another for service. As long as there is at least one teacher, God's will for togetherness and growth can be carried out. *You* may have to be that teacher.

If you have been given a talent by God to equip others, as a good steward of His gift you must use it to glorify God. Since equipping can't take place without togetherness, God wants you to be with other Christians so that you can

182

help build them up. In turn, other Christians will be building you up with their gift of equipping. Of course, like most spiritual gifts, we receive the fullest benefit from them when we share them or give them away to others.

There is one gift that we all have, and God specifically assembled us together for the purpose of sharing that gift. It's encouragement. We love to quote Hebrews 10:23-25, which says not to "forsake our own assembling together," and use it as a command for church attendance. The whole point of the Holy Spirit's admonition is for us not to miss an opportunity to give encouragement to others. People don't "skip church," they miss a chance to "stimulate one another to love and good deeds."

Somewhere, somehow we have to change our mind-set from what the church owes us to what we owe the church. As grateful grace-filled children of God, we submit, we support, and we serve. Satan has twisted our thinking around so much that we want our preferences, our opinions, and our needs to come first. *We assemble to give. We give love, encouragement, and a living picture of Jesus to all those who gather together with us.*

To all those who are in a spiritual tizzy about change in the assembly, I offer these two reminders. First, the church does not owe you security and predictability. I have told the story before about the elderly brother's plea that was made during an assembly planning meeting. He told about how his world had changed in every way since he came home from World War II. He listed all the areas that he'd lost confidence in and all the things that had disappointed him, and he concluded by saying, "The church is the last place where I can come and have the security of knowing that things aren't going to change."

It broke my heart and brought tears to my eyes. All I wanted to say was, "Brother, as far as I'm concerned our assemblies can go unchanged for as long as you live." I didn't say that, and I didn't say what needed to be said either. The church doesn't exist to provide security, nor is it the purpose of the assembly. That is not even remotely a reason for Christians to assemble. The feeling that the church owes us security and predictability is the result of a *me*-oriented perspective of the assembly.

The second reminder is for those on the flip-side of the change issue. The church doesn't exist, nor is it the purpose of the assembly, to provide you with excitement. That doesn't mean that it can't or won't happen in the assembly, but excitement is a state of mind. We are excited about grace, love, redemption, and heaven! We are excited about being with others who love us and are heaven-bound with us. If we have to have some external stimuli to get us excited about being children of God, then we've missed the point of getting together. Thinking the church owes you an exciting assembly is as *me*-oriented as the fear-of-change brother. It's creating a worldly criterion for judging the assembly, and it reduces togetherness to feel-good acts and adrenaline rushes. It's not reveling in love but reveling in rhythms and surprises. It's artificial, temporary, and totally subjective.

We can be excited about anything we choose to be excited about. If we are looking for things to be excited about, like meaningful prayers, beautiful lyrics, passionate words of encouragement, enthusiastic brethren, and a grateful heart, then we will find it. If we've made up our minds that everything is archaic, meaningless, or too different to enjoy, then we will never be happy.

Why can't it be enough that someone else is happy, touched, and uplifted by what happens? Why can't we be uplifted by the joy that others receive in the new songs or old songs that we don't particularly care for? At the risk of sounding like a heretic, I must confess that I don't particularly care for the hymn "How Great Thou Art." I think I got burned out singing it so much in college. It's also usually sung too slowly, and I feel like I'm walking in knee-deep mud while trying to finish it. But I love the fact that my brethren love it. I love the look on their faces as they sing out at the top of their voices and beam with praise. So I sing out loud and strong for them — not for me. After all, Paul said we are "teaching and admonishing one another" when we sing (Col 3:16). It doesn't have to be something I like or I would choose. We sing for one another not for ourselves! When others are uplifted, God is praised, and that is real worship.

BEING AN ASSEMBLY STEWARD

Whether or not your assembly is everything it's supposed to be or what you wish it would be is beside the point. You are a steward of everything God has given you and that includes the opportunity to be with the brethren you have chosen to fellowship with. Are they steeped in tradition? Have they not had a change since the day air conditioning was installed? Maybe it's a congregation on the cutting edge of change. They have new songs, power-point-projection, praise teams, and a snapping, fast-moving format. Do you like it? Do you hate it? It doesn't matter! The question is not whether or not you like everything that goes on, but are you there because of what you can give to others? Remember our precondition at the start of this chapter? How can we make the most of our assemblies regardless of what everyone else does?

What happens to you in the assembly of the saints is totally up to you. I have spent a lot of years studying, praying, preaching, and writing about worship. The fact that there is absolutely no biblical precedent for our present-day formalism, tradition-steeped, "one-hour-a-week" view of worship, doesn't seem to bother many people — even brethren who understand and agree with what I've preached and written. It amazes me! The New Testament is so obvious in its teaching of our life being worship to God, yet brethren still don't have any problems thinking of it as something they go to on Sunday morning. There is not a single example of a New Testament congregation in an assembly that remotely looks anything like what we do, yet we think what we do is copying a New Testament pattern. People are shocked and surprised to discover that the word "worship" is never once applied to the Christian assembly in the New Testament! I've had brethren respond with, "Well, how about that. Got to run. I'm late for worship."

My purpose here is not to review my previous two books on worship. I want all of us to understand that if we wait for the church, our brethren, to change their perspective on worship and the assembly before we decide to be good stewards, we will never be good stewards! We don't do any favors for God, our congregation, or ourselves by being disgruntled, self-righteous, or walking around with a chip on our shoulders because we know the truth and they don't. You may not have a better opportunity to be humble and submissive than when it comes to your attitude about the assembly. You are not going to change the church's thinking and traditions very much in your entire lifetime. That's fine, because your focus is on touching lives for Jesus. That means using every one-another event to accomplish what Christians are supposed to do for one another.

Decide today that the assembly is going to be your personal ministry of love. Get out of the spectator seat, the judge's chair, the pity pew, and decide that you are going to make the assembly an uplifting experience for as many people as you can. Guess what that will do for lifting you up?

I offer the following suggestions. These are not about assembly styles but assembly souls!

1. **Prepare yourself through prayer.** There's power in prayer (Jas 5:16-18). There is nothing that will revolutionize and revitalize a church's assembly time like every member praying for it prior to arriving. Prayer gets us in

the right mind-set and it focuses our attention on pleasing God not ourselves. Try having a brief prayer with your family before you leave home or praying in your car before you get out at the church building. Pray that God will use you to strengthen others. Pray that God will use those leading the assembly singing, praying, communing, and study. Pray that God will help you not to miss a single opportunity to represent Jesus properly.

2. **Prepare yourself to prey.** Become a hunter! Determine that you are going to seek out people to encourage. Prowl the halls and foyer! Stalk the aisles and pews! Arrive early to give yourself more time to find victims. Stick around afterwards and catch the ones you missed earlier. Think "others"! Greet your brethren with warmth, happiness, and positive encouragement! There is nothing more clearly taught in the New Testament than that the early church was BIG into greeting one another (1 Cor 16:20; 2 Cor 13:12; 1 Pet 5:14; 1 Thess 5:26). You are a greeter whether or not your congregation has an official Greeters Ministry or a time for Greeting during the assembly. Look for those who need special encouragement. Sometimes they are listed in your bulletin, but don't let that limit your opportunities. Watch peoples' faces. Look for sadness, depression, hurting, loneliness, and other struggles that brethren always have. Give them attention, give them words of comfort, give them hugs, and then send them a follow-up encouragement card. This transition from consumer to hunter will be one of the most thrilling experiences of your life.

3. **Focus on joy not judging.** This is going to be difficult, but it is possible. It's the way Jesus would approach the assembly. We need to replace our short fuses and long faces with "joy inexpressible and full of glory" (1 Pet 1:8). We need to throw away the score cards and replace the judges' robes "and clothe [ourselves] with humility toward one another, for God is opposed to the proud,

but gives grace to the humble" (1 Pet 5:5). Decide that you are going to enjoy everything that takes place when you are with your church family. The assembly should be one of the most joy-filled events of our life, but often it's far from it. That's okay! Don't depend on externals or permission from anyone else to make the assembly joyful for you. Look for things to appreciate and be grateful for. Smile at everything and everybody! Internalize each activity. Don't miss an opportunity to learn, grow, confront inadequacies, or build up others. Praise God for every song, prayer, and Scripture. Truly give cheerfully (2 Cor 9:7). Don't let any activity that you choose to participate in become an act of self-righteousness because you're doing it to be seen by man or to have something to judge others by. It's amazing how things as simple as where you sit, whether you open your Bible or even carry one, whether you clap to a song or raise "holy hands" before the Lord, or even if you say "Amen," can become criteria for judging others' faithfulness. Don't allow yourself to think like that! "Rejoice in the Lord always; again I will say, rejoice" (Phil 4:4).

4. **Be vocal.** God gave you a voice, He commanded you to encourage others, and He provided the opportunity with the assembly. How can we dare ignore all that He has done to make sure we lift up one another? Sing with all your heart! Love it! Sing for others' edification and strengthening not just your own enjoyment. Visit and encourage others every second you can. In some congregations there's more one-another action in the aisles and foyer before and after "the formal worship" than during it. Look for reasons to say "Amen." If it's not customary or permissible at your congregation, say it to God!

5. **Be physical.** No, I'm not talking about rolling in the aisles or climbing on top of the pews. However, put your whole body into what you do. Stop settling down

188

in your pew and using a songbook to prop up your arm and head. Remove as many distractions as you can by sitting up front. Try sitting on the front of your seat, at least some of the time. You do it at basketball and football games when you're really "caught up" in the game. Decide you're going to be "caught up" in the assembly. Sit up, sit forward, and don't be afraid to move. Slide forward and bow, or kneel when you pray. Lean on the pew in front of you. (Just don't breathe down the neck of the person sitting there.) Take notes on the sermon, write down reminders and passages of Scripture to check out later (Acts 17:11). Add names to your list of those to encourage. Putting yourself physically into what you do will encourage others, set an example, and make it the fastest hour you've ever spent in your life. You'll wish it were longer and realize that you never checked your watch once during the entire assembly time.

6. **Be Jesus for others.** That shouldn't be a scary proposition. We are supposed to be Christlike wherever we are. Surely we can be Christlike during an assembly that's held in His name. We all feel unworthy and inadequate for the task of representing Jesus, but that seems to be especially true when we are gathered together with His church. We are all the same. We are all struggling. At the same time, we all need to see Jesus in one another. I believe that is part of the providential work of God. He uses others to guide us, inspire us, and teach us. God will use you to reach others with His will, and you may never be aware of it. So I'm not talking about sitting in a pew and having some halo illuminated over your head. I'm talking about others seeing the love of Jesus in your life, your face, and in your concern for them. This is also important from the standpoint of our remembering how illogical and unspiritual it is for us to be un-Christlike when we don't like something that happens in the assembly. I've seen Christians furious because something

different happened. Not unbiblical — just different! Would Jesus have been red-faced furious over something different — something that did not violate Scripture? We can't declare, like Paul did, that "for to me, to live is Christ, and to die is gain," and then act like the devil when we're with the brethren (Phil 1:21). Asking ourselves over and over again in the assembly, "What would Jesus do?" is a wonderful way to stay focused on Him and make the most of the opportunity.

7. **Follow through and follow up.** Remember that the assembly is only one part of our opportunities to worship, not the entire worship experience. Thank God for the experience and the opportunity to touch and be touched by so many wonderful brethren. Follow up on all the things for which you have written notes. Pray for those who need prayers, send cards to those who need cards, and reflect on how God used you to carry out His will. Do some soul-searching to see how you can be a better steward of the assembly in the future.

Perspective is everything. We decide how we want to view things. When things can't or won't change, we are left with the only other viable alternative, which is to change our perspective. That is not only the way we must deal with much of life's stresses, but it's also how we keep Satan from turning a struggle into a barrier. Satan loves it when brethren stay in a constant state of turmoil over which style of assembly they ought to have.

Our perspective will not change until we recognize that the assembly is a communion to be built, not a commodity to be consumed. The focus of our assembly is Jesus, but He tells us the way we focus on Him is to love one another and be compassionate (Matt 25:31-46; John 21:15-17). We have to change the way we think about the assembly.

Proverbs tells us "For as he thinks within himself, so is he" (23:7). If we think of our assembly as something done for us, to make us feel good and happy, then selfish thinking will make us selfish people. If, on the other hand, we think of the assembly as an opportunity to serve others, to give encouragement, and to share Jesus, then "loving thinking" will make us loving people. The world will then know that we are His disciples, because they will see the love we have for one another. That is what being a good steward is all about.

DISCUSSION QUESTIONS

1. What does the church owe you?

2. Whose responsibility is it to make the assembly meaningful?

3. Which is more important to you: being uplifted by the assembly or helping someone else to be uplifted in the assembly?

4. How can we make the most of our assembly regardless of what everyone else does? What does that mean?

5. What are some ideas for making your assembly more "one-another" oriented?

CHAPTER TWELVE
Stewards of Our Victory

In the early 1990s I purchased an Isuzu Rodeo™. I was living in Texas and wanted to drive something that sounded rugged, western, and American. So I bought a Japanese-made SUV (sports utility vehicle). This was just before owning an SUV became as popular as it is today, so I was able to garner a lot of stares and envious comments. Actually, while it looked really rugged and sporty, it was only a two-wheel drive, small truck with the back enclosed. It was rugged in its suspension system and I felt it . . . even on good roads. Especially since I'd spent the previous four years driving a Buick Park Avenue™. I used to compare the two vehicles by saying that the Park Avenue™ was like riding a really great thoroughbred horse, while the Rodeo™ was like being dragged by a rope that was attached to a really good thoroughbred horse.

It was fun to drive and it met all my in-city and hunting needs. It had two buttons on the panel between the two front seats that were a mystery to me for a long time. One was marked with "Power" and the other with "Winter." I probably should have read the owner's manual to see what they did, but "real men" don't need to read manuals, maps, or THE directions — right?

I figured out that the power button was a passing gear. It gave you a little extra boost if you needed to get around someone in a hurry. The other, I figured, had to do with driving on ice, which in mid-Texas wasn't a huge concern.

There was a small patch of mud on the property where my associate minister and I hunted. It was smack-dab in the middle of the old farm road. It could be circled, but why do something like that when you are driving an SUV? So, I drove out into the mud slick and immediately got stuck. It wasn't deep, just slick, and everything I tried just made one of the tires spin, which of course made the other tire slip out of traction and become worthless.

Well, it was my vehicle and I was the "senior minister," so my associate, Cary Branscum, got out to do some pushing. Besides, he was bigger than I was, and I knew he'd do a much better job. He started pushing and I hit the gas. He got covered with mud, but with determination we got ourselves unstuck. Later that afternoon, while we were resting up for an evening of hunting, Cary came over to me with the Rodeo™ manual in his hands. He was a little put-out as he explained to me what that "Winter" button did. It seems it engages the positive traction on the Rodeo™, which greatly improves its ability to *keep* from getting stuck or to *get out* of being stuck. We had many good laughs for many years about the importance of reading the directions.

Every one of us is on a spiritual journey. We are "strangers and exiles on the earth . . . seeking a country of [our] own" (Heb 11:13-14). We are travelers with a great treasure — the saving grace of Jesus Christ, and "we have this treasure in earthen vessels, that the surpassing greatness of the power may be of God and not from ourselves" (2 Cor

4:7). But because we are earthen vessels, we sometimes get stuck in the mud. It's not always the mud of rebellion, sin, and wickedness. Occasionally it's the mud of inactivity, burnout, rut-religion, or lost vision. Whatever the cause, we're still stuck in the mud — not going, growing, and glowing like we should. We can't be good stewards of all that God has given us if we remain stuck in the mud. We may think that we are worshiping God because our mud-seat is a comfortable pew, but the only one impressed is Satan. He loves it when children of God think spinning tires in the mud is the same thing as spiritual progress.

Praise God, we don't have to stay in that mud slick! Not only does God offer forgiveness for His children on a constant basis (1 John 1:7), He provides us with a clear focus, or vision of what we need to do. That has been the message of this book! We live to worship God with all that we are and have! We do this by being good stewards of everything He has given us, which means that it must all glorify Him. That is our purpose — our vision — our "living and holy sacrifice, acceptable to God, *which is* [our] spiritual service of worship" (Rom 12:1).

Sometimes we forget that God wants us to be spiritually victorious. We can't be victorious without His enabling power working within us. However, He won't automatically give us something we don't want. He wants victory for us! Do we want victory for ourselves? God isn't "wishing for any to perish but for all to come to repentance" (2 Pet 3:9). He "causes all things to work together for good to those who love" Him, and He wants all of His children to "overwhelmingly conquer through Him who loved us" (Rom 8:28 and 37). It is "God, who gives us the victory through our Lord Jesus Christ" (1 Cor 15:57). Are we willing to refocus with His vision and accept His victory?

In the closing pages of this book, I want us to examine what it takes for us to move from vision to victory. What is involved in our going from stuck-in-the-mud Christians with a holy hobby to victorious, joyful stewards, who glorify God with every breath and thought our bodies and spirits produce?

The road from vision to victory involves understanding . . .

WHERE YOU'VE BEEN!

You already know where you've been — stuck in the mud! We get stuck in the mud when we don't pay attention to where we are going and we don't keep our momentum moving forward when we hit it. We don't wake up one morning and decide to get stuck in the mud. We are usually surprised to find ourselves in it. "Where did this come from?" We scream, "How did I get stuck in this mess?"

We become like a guy we have all read about in the Bible. Remember this story?

> And He said, "A certain man had two sons; and the younger of them said to his father, 'Father, give me the share of the estate that falls to me.' And he divided his wealth between them. And not many days later, the younger son gathered everything together and went on a journey into a distant country, and there he squandered his estate with loose living.
>
> Now when he had spent everything, a severe famine occurred in that country, and he began to be in need. And he went and attached himself to one of the citizens of that country, and he sent him into his fields to feed swine. And he was longing to fill his stomach with the pods that the swine were eating, and no one was giving *anything* to him (Luke 15:11-16).

Here is a guy who ended up stuck in the mud, and he clearly didn't start out thinking that that was where he'd end up. We are all very familiar with the story of the Prodigal son, but did you ever think that it was applicable to you? It's a classic "other guy" story! You know, Jesus was talking about everyone else and not you. You could never be like the Prodigal because you've never done anything that drastic — right? We all need to remember that mud, whether it's in a pigpen or not, is still mud wherever you find yourself stuck. We don't have to go to "a distant country" to find it. It could be in our own house.

Notice some of the steps to the mud that the Prodigal took. First, he wanted his share of the estate now not later. He didn't believe that "good things come to those who wait." He wanted "good times, wild living, and happiness," and he knew that with his share of the money, he'd have it all. How many of us have slid down that slope of impatience, greed, and materialism? It demands time, energy, and total focus, which means that there's often not time for family and God. Oh, we squeezed in church attendance at least once a week, but "things" and "good times," we thought, would truly bring happiness and fulfillment. Splat! (That's the sound of a Christian hitting mud.)

Of course, if you're going to change your priorities and focus on self, you have to get away from those who would be disappointed by your actions. The Prodigal went to a distant country where family and friends wouldn't see what he was doing. We just stop fellowshiping with those who might influence us to refocus on God. We stop attending the assembly, or at least cut it down to the bare minimum, stop serving with any ministry program, and stop hanging around with Christians in our social life. Splat!

Like the Prodigal, we squander what we've been given. Talents are buried, gifts go unused, and blessings are ignored. Stewardship is replaced by selfishness, and glorifying God is pushed aside by the pursuit of worldly success. Splat!

"Loose living" is usually thought of as sexual promiscuity, especially since his older brother declared that the Prodigal had spent his father's money "with harlots." It's really more a description of a change in values. He decided that he wanted to be worldly as opposed to godly, but he didn't want anyone back home to see him making these bad choices. When we rationalize away our need to be Christlike at all times, our need to be lights in a world of darkness, and our need to think of things true, honest, right, pure, lovely, of good repute, excellent, and praiseworthy, then we have changed our values as Christians. We buy into the lure of "loose living." It may be because we want acceptance, or feel it's a hazard of the job, or maybe we just want what Satan has to offer. Whatever the reason — Splat!

When everything was used up, all the "fair-weather friends" gone, and he was nearly at rock bottom with all his plans and ideas shattered, the Prodigal sought help, comfort, and solutions by attaching "himself to one of the citizens of that country." Completely ignoring family and friends back home, he reached out for help from someone who was more than happy to give him the final push into the pigpen and the mud. What looked so good and so promising to a young man who thought he knew better than his father finally led to his association with a pusher and his pigs. For us, they may be dressed in expensive suits and driving BMWs™, and seem to "really have it all together," but if they push you deeper into the mud and farther from your Father, they're pushers and pigs! Splat!

I have often thought that the saddest phrase in the entire story is "and no one was giving anything to him." That's the way it is in a dog-eat-dog world (or pig-eat-pig world). You find out that everyone is only out for themselves, and if that means stabbing you in the back and giving you a huge shove deeper into the mud, then that's the way it has to be. Only family, physical or spiritual, give without concern for anything in return. Corporate America and the world of financial success are populated by people who give nothing and take everything. To blend in, to succeed in that world, you usually have to become a taker too. Splat!

Now that you understand where you've been, the road from vision to victory next involves understanding . . .

WHERE YOU BELONG!

All three of my children are adults now. My youngest will be twenty within three months of this writing. It's hard to believe that I am old enough to have three adult children. I barely feel like an adult myself.

The last three years I have been doing a great deal of preaching and teaching about marriage, family, and parenting. I have especially enjoyed spending some time with our Young Families Class, which is made up of couples with small children. I want to share my knowledge and experience about parenting with them while all my failures and successes are still fresh on my mind. There have been plenty of things that I've shared that began with, "If I had it all to do over again, I'd do this differently." There are also plenty of things that I wouldn't change at all.

One of the things that I wish I could change but it's impossible to change is to take away any pain that my children suffered when they were small. Oh I know that pain is necessary and even good. It's God's warning system that something is wrong. I even wrote about that in my book *Life's Cobwebs* in a chapter about dealing with health problems. Still, when one of our children suffers, we'd gladly take his or her pain on ourselves if it were in any way possible.

My three children went through their share of cuts, bruises, broken bones, minor surgeries, and growing pains. I'll never forget the pain my wife and I felt as our son screamed through having tubes put in his ears to drain them from infection. Years later, while on a mini-mission trip to Saudi Arabia, I had to hear from a distance that one of my daughters had accidentally cut her leg when I couldn't be there to help and comfort her. I will especially never forget standing in the emergency room and watching a doctor set my son's broken arm. He didn't feel much because of the painkillers given to him, but I felt every pull and twist by the doctor.

Back then, when they were young and immature, they didn't spend much time thinking about things from Mom and Dad's perspective. But now that they are away from home and on their own, they remember those experiences and realize how nice it was (and is) to be loved. They know that we will always love them no matter what happens. Home is a refuge, an emotional and spiritual resort, and a place of acceptance and forgiveness.

Things like that must have been going through the mind of the Prodigal as he munched on pods and smelled the pigs. The Bible says,

> But when he came to his senses, he said, "How many of my father's hired men have more than enough bread, but I am dying here with hunger! I will get up and go to my father, and will say to him, 'Father, I have sinned against heaven, and in your sight; I am no longer worthy to be called your son; make me as one of your hired men.'" (Luke 15:17-19).

Probably the most poignant phrase in the entire story is "he came to his senses." He realized that he didn't belong in a pigpen picking pods from the mud. He belonged in his father's house. He'd always known that, but it took his hitting bottom to realize how high he had been. The key to helping him with that revelation was when he recognized his situation and declared, "I'm dying!"

There is the obvious lesson for us of dying in sin when we are separated from the Father. But look at it literally. I am dying. You are dying. Not spiritually, because we are saved by the blood of Jesus, but physically we have been dying since the day we took our first breath. We've always thought of it as something "way off in the future," but more than likely, you and I are closer to our death than to our birth. It's really going to happen to all of us. One of these days the coffin will have our body in it and there will be no more mornings or evenings, days or nights, because time will be no more. Of course, if we are redeemed by Jesus, there will also be no more pain, sickness, dying, or tears. We will be with God, Jesus, and all the saints who have gone before us — in heaven.

Few things are more sobering and help us focus on where we belong as the realization that we are dying. You may not have cancer, a heart condition, or some terminal disease — yet — but you're still dying. Do you realize where you belong?

Closely connected to understanding our mortality is our recognition of sin. The Prodigal, realizing that he belonged with his father, also realized that he was a sinner and unworthy of his father's forgiveness. The attitude of a broken heart is clearly seen in his cries, "I have sinned" and "I am no longer worthy to be called your son." This came from reflecting on how wonderful and loving his father was as compared with his own selfishness and sinful living. How could such a holy father possibly accept and forgive such an unholy son?

We know that we belong with the Father and that only He can lead us to the victory we long for. But we're sinners. We are convicted, hopeless, and helpless, but He loves us and saves us in spite of us (Rom 5:5-11). We don't and never will deserve such love and grace, so we will always be unworthy. Like the Prodigal, the road to victory includes our willingness to be a servant, because we are unworthy to be called sons. That's just fine because we know where we belong.

That means that the road from vision to victory must also include understanding . . .

WHOM TO PLEASE!

I love preaching God's Word! In nearly thirty years of preaching, I've had very few times when I doubted that it was what God wanted me to do. Most of those few times came in the early years when I was learning and growing and making plenty of mistakes. I look forward to every preaching opportunity. God's Word excites me and I can't wait to share what He has allowed me to learn. It's fun, challenging, and immensely rewarding. I've never had "just a job" and I never have "gone to work" or "left work." I am what I do!

It's easy, however, for a preacher to conclude that preaching is a "no win" occupation. It is impossible to please all the brethren all the time, but of course, that is not the purpose of preaching anyway. Yet, we all like to be liked. We enjoy compliments, praise, and pats on the back as much as anyone does. The problem is that everyone has his or her own idea of what the preacher ought to say and how he ought to say it.

Through the years I have received plenty of encouragement and support. I don't have a fragile ego that breaks with every criticism and complaint. I pray for guidance and direction. I study and I'm prepared for everything I do. So I've learned to relax and take the barbs in stride because I'm comfortable with how the Holy Spirit has led me.

I've received just about every kind of criticism you could imagine. I've used the wrong word, the wrong illustration, the wrong passage, and the wrong topic. I've had too much, too little, been too loud, too soft, too pushy, too soft on sin, too rough on toes, and been too general and too specific. I've dressed wrong, moved too much, worried about the clock too much, ignored the clock too much, picked on people, had too much Scripture and not enough Scripture, and I've worried people by standing on the edge of the podium. I've been inappropriate, irrelevant, illogical, unscriptural, emotional, dull, boring, dramatic, threatening, and sarcastic. (And all that was just last week!)

While doing a worship seminar in the North not long ago, I was talking about people who have fussed at me over semantics. I've been corrected for saying that Jesus "spilt" His blood, because (according to one brother) spilling is an accident and Jesus died on purpose. Another brother got really upset over a communion presider saying "the broken body of Jesus" because the Scriptures clearly taught that none of Jesus' bones were broken — just like the prophecy said. I guess he'd never heard of flesh being broken (besides, who could eat Jesus' flesh and drink His blood in one bite or gulp?–John 6:35).

Right after the very sermon where I'd mentioned these things, a nice sister came up to me and criticized me for referring to "Bible stories." She said that stories are fiction and the Bible is fact. I thanked her, but I wanted to say, "Did you ever see 'The Greatest Story Ever Told?'"

Please understand, these kinds of things are far and few between. Like I said, I receive more than enough support and "strokes" from loving brethren. But even if I didn't, I'm old enough and weathered enough to handle it. The key for me is the understanding that God is the One who must be pleased with my preaching. If my conscience is clear with Him, then everything else is secondary.

This is what the Prodigal finally discovered. Life was not about "gusto," "kicks," and "good times." It's not about pleasing others who have no desire to glorify God, even if they do own the farm. Life is about pleasing the One who loves us, forgives us, and saves us. So,

> he got up and came to his father. But while he was still a long way off, his father saw him, and felt compassion *for him,* and ran and embraced him, and kissed him. And the son said to him, "Father, I have sinned against heaven and in your sight; I am no longer worthy to be called your son." But the father said to his slaves, "Quickly bring out

the best robe and put it on him, and put a ring on his hand and sandals on his feet; and bring the fattened calf, kill it, and let us eat and be merry; for this son of mine was dead, and has come to life again; he was lost, and has been found." And they began to be merry (Luke 15:20-24).

Like a lot of us, the Prodigal didn't realize how good he had it until he didn't have it anymore. In the mire of mud he remembered what a wonderful and loving father he had. He began to focus on him and not himself. He began to think about making him happy. So he got up and headed for his father.

Isn't it interesting that the Bible doesn't say anything about the son being surprised to find his father waiting and looking for him? That's because he wasn't surprised at all. He knew his father would be looking for him because that was the kind of person his father was!

How many times each day had the father walked out to the front of the house and looked down the road for his son? How many prayers had he offered up to God on his behalf? Just imagine the ache, the longing to know about him, and the constant concern for his welfare that the father had during all that time. His love and concern was genuine, humble, and guileless. We know that because of the way he reacted when he finally did see his son coming down the road.

He didn't announce to everyone, "Well, here he comes . . . finally. I knew he would when he ran out of money!" Without a word he ran to meet him while he was still a long way off. The reaction of the father is what signaled everyone else that the son had returned. No one else cared like the father did.

How long has our Father waited for you to return? The whole purpose of this story that Jesus told was to help us understand God and His love for us. We have all been off in a far country wasting His blessings, and He wants us back home. In this story we see His tenderness, His hurt, His longing for reconciliation, and His desire to extend forgiveness. We also see His persistence. He's been waiting a long time, and He'll keep on waiting until time is no more. Then it will be too late to move from the pigpen to the mansion prepared by Jesus.

And how does the Father react when one of His children comes home? Party time! This Godlike father in Jesus' story calls for a robe, a ring, and sandals for his boy, and throws a huge barbecue where everyone is ordered to eat and be merry. God is excited when a child of His goes from being lost to being found. Angels rejoice and everything spiritual celebrates, because souls are so important. This image of rejoicing and feasting is a far cry from singing a verse of "Oh Happy Day" and then dismissing the congregation to the Luby's™ of their choice. When someone goes from dead to alive — it's a big deal to God!

This particular part of Jesus' story is remarkable for a couple of reasons. It not only shows us that reconciliation is very important to God — worth celebrating and rejoicing in a big way — but it also shows us that our Father is emotionally affected by it. Just as the father was "merry," so God is merry or happy when one returns to Him. Our mental image of a stern-faced, white-bearded, old man, sitting on a marble throne, totally unaffected by what He sees, isn't the God of the Bible. Our God, like His Word, is "living and active" (Heb 4:12). He has feelings and emotions, which are seen and described all through the Bible. He hurts, He rejoices, and He longs for reconciliation with His children. When it happens, He's just as happy and thrilled as the father Jesus talked about in His story.

It's great to realize that we have such a Father. It makes us want to please Him even more just as Jesus did. In John 8:28-29 He declared,

> When you lift up the Son of Man, then you will know that
> I am *He*, and I do nothing on My own initiative, but I
> speak these things as the Father taught Me. And He who

sent Me is with Me; He has not left Me alone, for I always do the things that are pleasing to Him.

That's what good stewards do, they please their Master. His will becomes more important than our own, and pleasing Him becomes more important than pleasing anyone else. This must be an absolute that we live by, because the road from vision to victory also involves understanding . . .

NOT EVERYONE'S EXCITED!

He was tired, worn out, and unappreciated. He put in a long hard day of working, and was now walking back to the house to eat a quiet dinner and go to bed. As he came over the rise behind the house, he heard music, laughter, and dancing coming from the house. There was a celebration going on and no one told him or invited him. While he was out there sweating and putting calluses on his calluses, they were having a party! He picked up his pace and felt a slow boil begin in his stomach.

As he got closer to the house he called one of the servants over and demanded an explanation. The servant told him about his brother's return and how his father was so overjoyed that he called for a feast to celebrate his return. This caused the boil to become an explosion.

> But he became angry, and was not willing to go in; and his father came out and began entreating him. But he answered and said to his father, 'Look! For so many years I have been serving you, and I have never neglected a command of yours; and yet you have never given me a kid, that I might be merry with my friends; but when this son of yours came, who has devoured your wealth with harlots, you killed the fattened calf for him (Luke 15:28-30).

In reality, he had been in a "distant country" too. It's just that his "distant country" was a lot closer to home. He had been on a journey of selfishness, squandering his relationship with his father, and wallowing in the pigpen of jealousy. He had the same loving, tender, and patient father as the Prodigal; he just hadn't come "to his senses" yet like his brother had.

If the older brother had learned from his father what he should have learned, he'd have been as excited to see the Prodigal brother as his father was. It must have been painful to the returning brother to see the anger, jealousy, and pride of his brother. But then, he'd realized that pleasing his father is what counted most. The one who was hurt the most was the father.

As he walked out to his son, just as he did with the Prodigal, he could see the anger and pouting clearly on his face. It must have been a terrible disappointment to him. The saddest phrase in the story is "his father came out and began entreating him." There's something out of place for such a father to have to "entreat" his son to join the celebration. Can you image making God say, "Please," before you agree to do His will?

That's exactly what He did for us. "Please" is simply an expression of kindness. God sent His only Son to die on a cross in order that we might have eternal life (John 3:16). Isn't that a lot better and stronger than saying, "please?" God entreats us to come back to Him. He wants us to join in with the rejoicing of those who are saved. What more does He have to do to convince us that He wants us back?

In the *New American Standard Bible*, the son's first word is "Look!" This is a very accurate translation of the Greek and clearly signifies "a disrespectful attitude toward his father" (v. 15). What followed was an attack on his father and brother that showed a long-term discontentment, jealousy, and smoldering anger. His loyal service and obedience had never been rewarded with a steak dinner. In other words, his expectations of what the father should have done for him were not fulfilled. Yet, the father pointed out that he could have had anything he wanted any time he wanted it because "all that is mine is yours."

I am especially drawn to his rationale that he deserved more because he "never neglected a command." He never sinned, broke a command, or did anything wrong! But because he never had the right heart, he never realized how loving and gracious his father was and therefore never enjoyed the blessings that were his for the taking.

Isn't it strange that the one who never left ended up being farther away from his father than the one who had journeyed to a far country?

There will always be the "I never" types around to let you know that they are "holier than thou." They grumble, judge, criticize, warn, threaten, and condemn. They like acts of righteousness and fruits of repentance to be determined by them. They may be older, harder workers, and have tenure (at least in their own minds), but they are not any closer to the Father than you are. They rob visions and create barriers on the road to victory. Listen to the Father not them. He is the one who took you from where you were to where you belong, back in His house. He is the One you are to please, not the "older brothers" who are long on law and short on grace.

Our Father seeks reconciliation with His children. He planned for it from the foundation of the earth. When we go from being lost to being found, from being dead to being alive, His hopes and dreams are fulfilled. That's why the father in the story told the older brother, "But we had to be merry and rejoice"(v. 32). It is the nature of our Father to be happy when we do His will. There will always be some who don't know the meaning of "be merry and rejoice," but our Father isn't one of them. As good stewards, if we make Him happy and keep Him happy by our obedience, those who don't understand or like it will have to work it out with God. He will entreat them, but He won't call off the celebration just because they don't "get it."

If we are serious about being good stewards, about pleasing our Heavenly Father, we must press on regardless of whatever anyone else does or says. We must be totally and consistently His children, and not skipping back and forth between His house and the "distant country."

"THERE'S NO PLACE LIKE HOME!"

Not long ago I left the church building to go home for the day. As I started backing my truck out of the parking space, I noticed a small spider on the hood. I stopped for a few seconds to see if it would jump off, and when it didn't, I decided to ignore it and let the wind take care of things. It was still there when I got to the end of the parking lot. As I turned onto Antioch Pike and accelerated up to about thirty-five miles per hour, it never moved. When I turned onto Haywood Lane and picked up speed to enter the Interstate, it never moved. As I exited onto I-24, I just knew it would only be a matter of time before the 65-mph wind blew it away. It didn't. It rode all the way to my house, the full 6.5 miles, and was still there as I pulled into my driveway. Just before I pulled into my garage, it hopped off the hood and into my front yard. It was just as if it had planned it that way.

I told my family that it didn't talk or make any demands. It was just along for the ride. If we don't have a passionate desire to live totally for our Father — then we are like that spider, attached to the church just for the ride. In Jesus' classic story about the Prodigal son, He's really pointing out that both brothers were "just along for the ride" in terms of their relationship with their father. When the Prodigal left home, hit bottom, and "came to his senses" about how wonderful he'd had it in his father's house, he returned to a loving, forgiving, and joyous relationship. The other brother, was still "just along for the ride."

How many church folks are "just along for the ride"? They have no sense of gratitude or joy over being included in the Body of Christ. They contribute nothing but have strong opinions about how everything ought to be done. They're hot about change and cold about growing. To them, worship is something that you attend, watch, critique, and protect; stewardship is a token check in the collection plate; and total Christianity is for red-faced fanatics. For them, vision is being able to see from the back pew, and victory is having the songs they like in the praise service.

Stewardship isn't, never was, and never will be a matter of what goes into the contribution plate on Sunday morning. That's a man-made and unbiblical perspective on stewardship that has been used by many for capital gains, production of guilt, and institutionalizing giving.

We are stewards! Everything given to us by God, whether material or spiritual, must be used by us to glorify Him! We are stewards by His grace. That means that all of it is free, undeserved, and out of love. Everything given to us is given to be given away and shared, because that is what stewards of God, who want to be like Him, do. Stewardship is worship because they both involve our being "a living and holy sacrifice." They are both total Christianity. They are both conditions of the heart that manifest themselves through consistent Christlike behavior. They are the result of a "life hidden with Christ in God" (Col 3:3). If our life isn't hidden with Christ, we can fill the offering basket with checks and cash every Sunday, but our life will be an *empty basket* before God.

DISCUSSION QUESTIONS

1. Why do so many Christians not feel "victorious" in their spiritual walk with God?

2. The story of the Prodigal in Luke 15 is a parable. What are some contemporary "pigpens" in which people find themselves today?

3. What does this story teach us about our heavenly Father?

4. Looking at your own life, when do you most feel that you are pleasing God? Why?

5. Is our Father waiting for you to return? How long has He been waiting? How long will you make Him wait?

Endnotes

1. *The Expositor's Bible Commentary*, Vol.10 (Romans–Galatians) (Grand Rapids: Zondervan, 1976), p. 127.

2. Ibid.

3. William Barclay, *The Letter to the Romans*, The Daily Study Bible Series (Philadelphia: Westminster, 1975), pp. 156-157.

4. Ibid.

5. Ibid., p. 158.

6. *The Expositor's Bible Commentary*, p. 128.

7. Barclay, *Romans,* p. 158.

8. *The Expositor's Bible Commentary*, Vol. 12 (Hebrews–Revelation), p. 143.

9. Paul Lee Tan, *Encyclopedia of 7700 Illustrations* (Rockville, MD: Assurance Publishers, 1979), p. 289.

10. Ibid., p. 1526.

11. *The Expositor's Bible Commentary*, Vol.10, p. 224.

12. Tan, *Illustrations,* p. 297.

13. Ibid.

14. J.W. McGarvey, *Acts of Apostles* (Delight, AR: Gospel Light, 1863), p. 81.

15. *The Expositor's Bible Commentary*, Vol.8 (Matthew, Mark, Luke), p. 985.

Bibliography

Barclay, William. *The Letter to the Romans*. The Daily Study Bible Series. Philadelphia: Westminster Press, 1975.

The Expositor's Bible Commentary. Volumes 8, 10, & 12. Grand Rapids: Zondervan, 1976.

Mc Garvey, J.W. *Acts of Apostles*. Delight, AR: Gospel Light Publishing Company, Reprint from 1863.

Tan, Paul Lee. *Encyclopedia of 7700 Illustrations*. Rockville, MD: Assurance Publishers, 1979.

FOR FURTHER STUDY

Allen, Ronald, and Gordon Borror. *Worship: Rediscovering the Missing Jewel*. Portland, OR: Multnomah, 1982.

Couey, Richard B. *Building God's Temple*. Minneapolis: Burgess, 1982.

Kendrick, Graham. *Learning to Worship as a Way of Life*. Minneapolis: Bethany House, 1984.

MacArthur, John. *The Ultimate Priority: John MacArthur on Worship*. Chicago: Moody Press, 1983.

Martin, Ralph P. *Worship in the Early Church*. Grand Rapids: Eerdmans, 1964.

Root, Mike. *Spilt Grape Juice: Rethinking the Worship Tradition*. Joplin, MO: College Press, 1992.

_____. *Unbroken Bread: Healing Worship Wounds*. Joplin, MO: College Press, 1997.

Taylor, Jack R. *The Hallelujah Factor*. Nashville: Broadman, 1983.

Webber, Robert E. *Worship Old and New.* Grand Rapids: Zondervan, 1982.

White, James F. *Protestant Worship, Tradition in Transition.* Louisville: Westminster/Knox Press, 1989.

Wiersbe, Warren. *Real Worship.* Nashville: Oliver Nelson, 1986.